GOALS

Gianluca Vialli is a husband and father who once played football for a living, later managed Chelsea and Watford, and then went on to become a successful television pundit.

He won league titles and European trophies, playing for world-famous clubs like Sampdoria, Juventus and Chelsea, as well as his hometown club, Cremonese. He represented the national team 59 times, played in two World Cups and in 2015 was included in Italian football's Hall of Fame.

Goals is Vialli's second book, following *The Italian Job: A Journey to the Heart of Two Great Footballing Cultures.*

Text translated by Gabriele Marcotti, author, senior writer at ESPN and correspondent for *Corriere dello Sport.*

Stories curated by Pierdomenico Baccalario and Gabriele Marcotti.

Also by Gianluca Vialli and Gabriele Marcotti

THE ITALIAN JOB

GIANLUCA VIALLI

GOALS

INSPIRATIONAL STORIES TO HELP
TACHLE LIFE'S CHALLENGES

Translated by Gabriele Marcotti

*Curated by Pierdomenico Baccalario
and Gabriele Marcotti*

HEADLINE

First published in Italy in 2018 by Mondadori Libri S.p.A., Milano

First published in Great Britain in 2020 by
HEADLINE PUBLISHING GROUP

First published in paperback in 2021 by
HEADLINE PUBLISHING GROUP

1

Cataloguing in Publication Data is available from the British Library

Paperback ISBN 978 1 4722 7490 8

Jacket design by Jack Storey
Jacket photograph © Charlie Compitus

Designed and typeset by EM&EN

Printed in Italy by Elcograf S.p.A.

Headline's policy is to use papers that are natural, renewable and recyclable
products and made from wood grown in well-managed forests and other
controlled sources. The logging and manufacturing processes are expected
to conform to the environmental regulations of the country of origin.

HEADLINE PUBLISHING GROUP
An Hachette UK Company
Carmelite House
50 Victoria Embankment
London EC4Y 0DZ

www.headline.co.uk
www.hachette.co.uk

For my family,
and for Ray

CONTENTS

AUTHOR'S NOTE

I love mantras and I love quotes. I constantly look for them. When I come across a good one, I write it down on a sticky note and attach it on one of the walls in my study.

I believe mantras are tools that make our thinking more effective. They are mental maps to be used to overcome stressful situations. More importantly, they are the best way to reveal the most profound meaning of a story, pass on the essence of a culture, and affirm a principle or a belief.

I like stories too. Real ones. In fact, I believe that connecting a great story to the right mantra creates a powerful and inspiring combination from which one can learn a great deal.

In my head it all started a while ago, well before I got unwell. A simple idea slowly upgraded to a goal which then turned into a proper project and eventually resulted in a book.

I really hope you will find the result a helpful guide for everyone who is dealing with a challenging situation, facing a tough test or fighting a struggle. Whether that is a job interview, a school exam, a heart break, a disease or that crucial moment when one has to make a call that will define one's future.

When we find ourselves at a crossroads and we don't know which path to choose, may the mantras in this book work like illuminating signposts, and may the stories be inspiring testimonies of everything human beings can achieve when travelling along their chosen paths.

I am not a 'real' author. *Goals* wouldn't have been published without the vision and expert guidance of Andrea Delmonte and Alberto Gelsumini at Mondadori, Jonathan Taylor at Headline and David Luxton, my literary agent. Their trust and courage to let me do almost everything I wanted has transformed this experience into an exciting and fulfilling journey (at least for me!).

They all believed that what I wanted to communicate was important and was worth investing time, energy and money in. By doing so, they put their reputation on the line.

I owe so much, too, to Gabriele and Pierdomenico for helping me to find, select and put down in words some of the most original, remarkable and inspiring true stories of sportswomen and sportsmen from the last couple of centuries.

The last three years of my life have been rather eventful. So much has happened. It has been demanding, both physically and mentally. I suspect I would not have survived the journey without the invaluable support of an amazing team led by my gorgeous wife, Cathryn; my darling daughters, Olivia and Sofia; my parents; my brothers and sister; my closest friends; Professor Cunningham and his incredible team of doctors and nurses at the Royal Marsden Hospital in Chelsea, as well as all the people who looked after me during the time I spent at the Humanitas Hospital in Milan. Thank you for sticking with me. I will be forever grateful.

My humble advice for the reader is quite simple: pick the book up and put it down as it pleases you. Read one, two or five stories at a time. Read the whole book in one go if you want to. Then let it sink in. Let it help with reshaping some of your convictions. Remember that our life is made

10 per cent by what happens to us and 90 per cent by the way we react to it; if we change the way we look at things, things begin to change.

Enjoy reading.

Gianluca Vialli
London, March 2020

GOALS

'QUOTES WON'T WORK UNLESS YOU DO.'

1

HELENIO HERRERA

He didn't particularly care about being liked. What drove Helenio Herrera was winning. And winning wasn't something that you started doing when you stepped on to the pitch. Nope; winning was something you did when you convinced yourself that you were going to succeed. Without that, there was no victory.

Born in Buenos Aires to a Spanish anarchist father and an Argentine mother, Herrera grew up in Casablanca in Morocco (which was then under a French protectorate). He spent his playing career in France, mostly at lesser clubs, topping up his wages by working as a door-to-door salesman, where his silver tongue made him a hit.

After retiring just after World War II, he went straight into management, first in France, then Spain, with a brief detour to Portugal. He was a man of the world, more than comfortable everywhere he went. He won two league titles at Atletico Madrid and another two (along with two Spanish Cups) at Barcelona, ultimately leaving after falling out with star player László Kubala.

Inter snatched him up and he moved to Milan. And it was here that the legend was born. Words, which were his currency, played a key role. Herrera stuck his aphorisms all over the club's dressing room and training ground. It was straightforward stuff:

'No obstacle must be an obstacle.'

'Talent + fitness + intelligence = league title.'

'If you play for yourself, you're playing for the opposition.'

As techniques go, it might sound corny today. But as one of Herrera's key players, Sandro Mazzola, put it, Herrera 'would train the mind first and the legs second'. The concepts stuck in the players' minds, both motivating them and building their trust in their manager.

That was half the battle: getting buy-in. There's no point having a brilliant tactical setup if the players don't believe in it and can't execute it. But Herrera had total loyalty, total belief. And it was thanks to his words.

The other half of the battle, of course, is what you actually do and who does it for you. Herrera excelled at persuading the club to invest in players he wanted. He would explain just how a player would fit in, why he may seem expensive but was actually a bargain, why nobody else could do the job the player was going to do. He also had the uncanny ability to make players think they were better than they actually were. He convinced Mauro Bicicli, a moderately gifted winger, that he was as talented out wide as the legendary Garrincha, in part by calling him that and whispering it in his ear before every game. And, sure enough, while Bicicli didn't quite perform at Garrincha's level, he certainly played well enough to make a real difference.

Herrera built a system of play which – while not particularly entertaining – proved to be extraordinarily effective: the '*Catenaccio*'. It was essentially a 5–3–2, with the sweeper behind and players sitting deep, creating density in front of their own goal. When they did win the ball back, they were lightning-fast in counterattacking.

And they could counter from anywhere. At a time when most teams' defenders focused mostly only on defending and, when they did win the ball, would simply pass it short to a midfielder, Herrera virtually created the position of attacking fullback. He turned Giacinto Facchetti into the

prototype of the modern fullback, a player capable of stopping opponents, sure, but also of bounding forward and
becoming an extra attacker when needed.

In some ways, Herrera was well ahead of his time. One
of his favourite sayings could be the mantra by which top
teams today play football: 'Think fast. Act fast. Play fast.'

His fans called him '*Il Mago*' or 'The Wizard'. His
critics, especially in Spain, said his initials, HH, really
stood for '*habla, habla*' or, 'talk, talk'. But the keys to his
success – which would see Inter win back-to-back European Cups – were precisely that: the things he said and the
words he chose.

'IF YOU QUIT ONCE
IT BECOMES A HABIT.
DON'T QUIT.'

2

FIORENZO MAGNI

When the 1956 Giro d'Italia set off from Milan, Fiorenzo Magni knew it could well be his final race. He was the defending champion, having won the Giro the year before aged thirty-four, becoming its oldest winner (a record that still stands today). But age was catching up with him – if it hadn't caught him already. All he wanted to do was finish the Giro, with a decent placing if possible.

He did better than expected in the early stages and, ever the fighter, maybe even mulled the possibility of springing a surprise attack or two in the Alps. But on 29 May, during the 230-kilometre stage from Grosseto to Livorno, he fell badly during a downhill stretch. He felt a strong pain in his left arm and, what's worse, he could hardly move it. The official race doctor caught up with him and his diagnosis was immediate.

'You've broken your collarbone, mate. You're done,' he said. 'You need to pull out.'

'I'll deal with it when I finish the stage,' Magni hissed, before mounting his bike. Somehow, he made it to the finish line.

The next day was a rest day and he spent most of it avoiding the doctor, who nevertheless found him and again insisted: 'You're done – don't even think about getting back on the bike.'

But after the doctor left, Magni got to work. He covered

his handlebars in foam rubber in an attempt to minimise the vibration of the bike, which caused waves of pain to race up his arm. And, sure enough, the next day, he was at the start line for the Livorno to Lucca time trial. Magni made it through another mountain stage, but at the next time trial, Bologna to Madonna di San Luca, the pain was so intense that he could not properly grip the handlebar.

He begged his mechanic, Faliero Masi, for help. Ever the outside-the-box thinker, Masi tied a rubber inner tube to the handlebar and gave Magni the other end to grip in his teeth. It enabled him to maintain some stability, but it made steering extremely difficult – and braking virtually impossible. Magni crashed again during a downhill stretch on the next stage, ending up in a ditch. He landed on his broken collarbone and fractured the humerus in his upper arm. The pain left him unconscious and he woke up in an ambulance bound for the hospital. He immediately demanded to be let out.

'You're mad! What are you doing?!' shouted the paramedic.

'Can't you see? I'm going to catch up with the peloton,' Magni said, climbing out of the ambulance. And sure enough, he forced himself back on the bike and re-joined the peloton, many of whom had slowed, concerned about his condition.

The next morning, unperturbed, rubber inner tube between his teeth, he was again at the start line as the Giro headed for the Alps. A few days later, came one of the most famous stages in Giro history: the 242-kilometre Merano to Monte Bondone stretch through the Dolomites. A freak blizzard and sub-zero conditions greeted the riders high up in the mountains, and more than sixty of them pulled out in a single day. All of them were younger and healthier than Magni that day. None of them had two broken bones in their body; none of them were steering up and down steep mountains with a rubber tube lodged between their teeth. But maybe that was it. Maybe, when you're already coping with such levels of pain, the discomfort caused by snow, ice and freezing conditions matters little.

Magni would go on to finish second in the Giro, behind Luxembourg's Charly Gaul, who himself had made one of the greatest comebacks in the history of the race. But in many ways, Magni's feat will stand the test of time more than Gaul's, and more than his three previous Giro victories. He stared physical pain in the face and overcame it, partly through ingenuity, and largely through sheer bloody-minded, refuse-to-quit willpower.

'LIFE IS 10% WHAT HAPPENS TO YOU AND 90% HOW YOU REACT TO IT.'

3

ALEX ZANARDI

Alex Zanardi lives to race. He can count himself fortunate to have been able to do it at the highest level in two different sports: motor racing and para-cycling. The daredevil attitude that made him excel in the former eventually led to the latter, and there's a certain irony in that.

Zanardi sailed through the different lower level competitions and was handed his first Formula One shot with Jordan back in 1991. He bounced from Jordan to Minardi to Lotus, failing to stick. Partly, it was his tendency to crash out. Partly it was bad luck, like when he was hit by a motorist while riding a bike in his hometown of Bologna, or when his car's suspension failed during practice for the Belgian Grand Prix in 1993, sending him against the barriers at 150 miles an hour. Such was the force of the blow on his lower spine that it left him more than an inch taller.

In 1995, he sought to make his own luck across the pond in the United States, joining a team in CART racing. He finished third overall in his third season and, perhaps as importantly, conjured up one of those manoeuvres that would live on in racing history forever. It was in Laguna Seca, the last race of the season, on a stretch of the circuit known as Corkscrew corner. To IndyCar racing fans, the manoeuvre became known simply as 'The Pass'. It was so daring and risky that it was subsequently banned. Go on and search for it on YouTube. We'll still be here when you get back.

Zanardi won back-to-back CART titles in 1997 and 1998. After a brief and unsuccessful return to Formula One with Williams, he returned to CART in 2001 and faced the moment that would change his life forever. It happened at the Lausitzring in Germany. Coming out of a pitstop with thirteen laps to go, he was heading to merge back into the race when he lost control of his car, accelerated abruptly and did a 180 across the grass and on to the track. Patrick Carpentier somehow avoided him, but the next driver, Alex Tagliani, crashed into him, impacting just behind the front wheel, right at the cockpit.

Zanardi was in a coma for four days. He would lose both his legs, as well as nearly three-quarters of his blood. Innumerable surgeries would follow. But his determination did not flag. He was fitted with prosthetic legs and announced he would return to racing. He spent years working with designers to create prosthetic legs that would allow him to race, while modifying cars so he could brake and shift with hand controls. And, eventually, he did. He raced some test cars for Sauber in Formula One and won races in the European Touring Car series.

He knew, however, that he could no longer compete at the very highest level in motorsports: Formula One. And so, he turned to para-cycling. After all, he was physically fit and insanely competitive – and it did not require the use of his legs. He entered the 2007 New York City marathon and finished fourth in the handcycling division, despite training for less than a month. He raced wheelchairs, winning marathons in Rome and Venice. He turned to triathlons, setting the Ironman world record for disabled athletes. And, of course, he excelled at the Paralympics, winning two golds and a silver in London and repeating the feat four years later in Rio.

That day at the Lausitzring he lost both his legs, but his competitive spirit was unscathed. And his determination and will to react and write his own story were only strengthened.

'BETWEEN STIMULUS AND RESPONSE IS OUR GREATER POWER: THE FREEDOM TO CHOOSE.'

4

JACKIE ROBINSON

It's easy to forget, but the United States Military was not officially desegregated until 1948, three years after black and white fought together side by side to liberate Europe from the grip of Nazi Germany. And, in fact, schools around the United States were not forcibly desegregated until 1955.

So perhaps it shouldn't be surprising that baseball, known as America's pastime, was also a segregated sport, right through World War II and its immediate aftermath. White Caucasian players turned out in Major League Baseball. Black players competed in the so-called 'Negro leagues'.

In 1945, a man named Happy Chandler became Commissioner of Baseball. He had been the Governor of Kentucky and had seen the damage segregation could do in his own state. Chandler recognised that the world was changing, and that sport needed to change with it.

'If [black Americans] can fight and die on Okinawa, Guadalcanal [and in] the South Pacific, they can play ball in America,' he famously said.

The problem was making it happen. Some team owners simply refused. Others, while open to the idea, feared repercussions among their own players and fans, as well as opposing supporters when their teams travelled to the Deep South, which was still in near-apartheid conditions.

Others still were enthused by the idea, not just from a moral perspective, but from a sporting and business one too: there were plenty of phenomenal athletes in the Negro leagues and some of those stars would instantly improve Major League teams.

One of those was Branch Rickey, president of the Brooklyn Dodgers. His concern, though, was finding the 'right' black player to integrate the league. It had to be somebody talented, sure, but also somebody tough-minded enough to deal with both the pressure and the abuse. And that wasn't easy.

Enter Jackie Robinson. On the surface, he wasn't an obvious choice. He was a hugely gifted athlete who had excelled at basketball and football, as well as winning a national long jump title in college. But he also had a burning intensity about him, a sense of right and wrong. And, potentially, a temper. In 1942 he had been drafted into the US Army, where he was court-martialled for refusing to sit at the back of the bus. It was a desegregated bus line and Robinson was in the right (he was later acquitted), but the way he stood up to the bus driver and the military prosecutor unnerved Rickey.

That's why, before allowing him to make his debut for the Dodgers, Rickey subjected Robinson to the sort of test that today seems utterly humiliating. Rickey greeted him with a barrage of racist epithets and insults, to see how he would react. It was critical to Rickey that the first black player in Major League Baseball be somebody who did not react to abuse but simply ignored it.

'Mr Rickey, are you looking for a Negro who is afraid to fight back?' Robinson asked him.

'No, I'm looking for a ball player with enough guts not to fight back.'

In some ways, what Rickey was looking for was a contradiction. It would take an enormously proud and strong-willed man to do what he was asking. And yet, at the same time, he was asking Robinson to bury that pride and will deep inside him, perhaps stoking his inner furnace, without ever letting it show. Few men could fit the bill, but Robinson did.

The two made an unspoken pact. Rickey would back him, and Robinson would not react to abuse. His mere presence and play on the field would change minds and attitudes.

It's hard to overstate what Robinson had to deal with in those first few years. Some of his teammates rebelled at his presence and Rickey had to threaten them so they would not interfere with Robinson's arrival. The Saint Louis Cardinals threatened to go on strike rather than play against a Dodgers team with Robinson in it. And he had to cope with the worst sort of racist insults from the stands, especially in the Deep South, where, on more than one occasion, black cats were thrown on to the field of play. To add to the indignity, when the Dodgers travelled to segregated cities, Robinson had to stay in a different hotel from his teammates and eat in different restaurants.

But the plan worked. By the end of that 1947 season, he was one of six Major League Baseball players of colour. By the end of the decade, there were eleven. And by the end of the 1950s, every single team had at least one black player.

It didn't mean racism was wiped out of baseball, of course. It did mean, though, that the trail had been blazed. And it was thanks to the courage and the discipline of number forty-two, Jackie Robinson.

'SO MUCH OF OUR HAPPINESS DEPENDS ON HOW WE CHOOSE TO LOOK AT THE WORLD.'

5

JAMAICA BOBSLEIGH FEDERATION

It all began with a soapbox race, of the sort that are popular in the hills of Kingston, Jamaica. George Fitch and William Maloney were businessmen with ties to Jamaica and, needing to kill time and wanting to do something 'different, but local', they opted to head over to the race. For those who don't know, soapbox racing consists of modifying wooden crates with wheels and ball-bearings, then throwing yourself down hills in them. One person steers and another person brakes, and that's about it. It's chaotic, it's breakneck and it can be the thrill of your life.

It struck Fitch and Maloney that there were obvious similarities to the bobsleigh. Pilot and brakeman sprint alongside the soapbox and then, at just the right split-second, jump in, holding on for dear life. Shame there was no bobsledding in Jamaica . . . no ice and snow either, for that matter.

Little by little, though, the idea didn't seem as mad as it first sounded. Jamaica, after all, was home to some of the world's greatest sprinters, young men who were fast and strong and coordinated. Surely they could learn to push the bob and get it on its way . . . then it would just be a question of steering.

Except the sprinters had little interest in these two Americans and their suggestion. So, Fitch and Maloney turned to the army: an excellent source of young, fit men.

An appeal to the patriotism of Colonel Ken Barnes did the rest. He delivered them a slew of potential recruits, including Devon Harris, a middle-distance runner and professional soldier. Devon did best in the trial and was handed the captaincy. With him were Dudley Stokes, from the air force, and an infantryman named Michael White. The only civilian was a railway engineer, Samuel Clayton, whose enthusiasm and technical knowledge proved invaluable.

How did they train? Why, on the soapboxes, of course! At least at first. Fitch proclaimed himself President of the Jamaican Bobsleigh Federation and set about raising money. He wangled an invitation for the team to train, first in Wyoming, then in Austria. They were treated like a novelty, sure, but they were also immensely likeable. Their catchy slogan – 'The Hottest Thing on Ice' – didn't hurt, either.

Stokes was chosen to pilot the sled. After all, he'd flown airplanes . . . how different could it possibly be? Rather different, as it happens. And, in fact, their time at an Austrian training camp saw them crash and spin out on a regular basis. They took it all in stride and their enthusiasm was infectious: so much so that Sepp Haidacher, a local Austrian coach, agreed to help them out. Standards improved enough for them to be invited to compete in the 1988 Calgary Winter Olympics, in both the four-man and two-man bobsleigh races.

The two-man bob, with Stokes piloting (cautiously) and White braking (often), saw them finish thirtieth. 'At least we didn't crash,' they told themselves. But, having spent most of their time training for the four-man bob, they approached this event with trepidation. Clayton was injured a few days before the race, and Stokes asked his brother, Chris (a sprinter who had hoped to make it to a different Olympics, the summer version in Seoul), to step in. Chris, who was only there to support his brother, accepted. With just three days' training, he took his spot on the team.

On race day, their first two runs were near-perfect. In fact, they had a chance of finishing in the top fifteen. Then, on the third run, while travelling at more than eighty miles an hour, Stokes lost control on a sharp turn, and the bobsleigh flipped. The irony is that he lost control because this was Jamaica's fastest ever start, and he had simply never steered at such speed. For twenty-five agonising seconds – which must have felt like much longer – they flew along the track upside down, their helmets and elbows scraping the ice. The gasps from the trackside crowd were audible; those from the worldwide television audience imaginable. Finally, the bobsleigh came to a halt. And, one after the other, Harris, White and the Stokes brothers extricated themselves. Their helmets came off. When they realised they were all OK, their faces broke out into smiles. They pushed their bobsleigh the rest of the way, which at that stage was just a few metres. They high-fived and shook hands with fans, but, make no mistake about it, they were disappointed – particularly Harris.

The impact of the occasion would only hit him years later.

'I've come to realise now that it meant so much more than just four black guys from Jamaica going to the Winter Olympic Games,' he said. 'It was really speaking to all those people across the world who I've met over the years who, in their own lives, wanted to go and chase their impossible dream as well, and never had the courage to do it.'

'In sporting terms, it was a failure,' he added. 'But sometimes success is not always about the final score.'

Thankfully not. Sometimes it takes on a far greater meaning.

'THE DISTANCE BETWEEN DREAMS AND REALITY IS CALLED ACTION.'

6

ALFONSINA STRADA

It's hard to overstate just how subversive and revolutionary the invention of the bicycle actually was. Suddenly, mobility was improved everywhere, at low cost – certainly lower than owning a horse. But the bicycle also became a symbol of empowerment. One of the earliest British suffragettes, Alice Hawkins, scandalised Leicester and drew attention to her cause by cycling around the centre of town – and doing so while wearing trousers, no less.

It was at around that time that Alfonsina Strada was born into a poor family in central Italy. Her father was a day labourer, her mother a nurse. Accounts vary of how many siblings she actually had, but there is no question that there were many. She was the second oldest and charged with looking after her younger siblings when she wasn't out in the fields, helping her father.

Outside of that, she spent every spare moment riding her father's bicycle as best she could. When she was around nine or ten, he brought home an old rusty bike, which, the story goes, he had acquired in exchange for some chickens. It was the happiest day of her life.

She rode that bicycle everywhere and as often as she could. Facts are hazy, but it is said that her family and local villagers frowned upon her enthusiasm for cycling and speed. Even her mother tried to dissuade her from it, while older folk would often cross themselves when she rode by.

Alfonsina entered as many races as she could, sometimes as a girl, sometimes – much to her parents' displeasure – tucking her hair under a cap and posing as a boy. Her enthusiasm and deep passion for cycling were alien to her family and they were relieved when they married her off to a man named Luigi Strada, who was ten years her elder.

If they hoped that Strada would quell Alfonsina's obsession with the bike, they were wrong. In fact, it only grew. For he too loved his bicycles, and his wedding present to her was a drop-handlebar racing bike. Her fame quickly grew to the point that, in 1909, Tsar Nicholas II of Russia invited her to Saint Petersburg to compete in a race.

Her dream was to compete in the Giro d'Italia, but despite repeated applications, she was routinely denied. Then, in 1924, there was a dispute between the organisers and the top riders of the day, who demanded to be paid an appearance fee in addition to prize money. The organisers of the Giro were concerned: without the big names, there was the real risk that interest in the race would diminish. As the story goes, they were figuring out how to respond when they noticed the application letter that Alfonsina had sent them every year for the past decade.

A metaphorical lightbulb lit up the room. *Let's have her race.* Even if it was just a publicity stunt, it would still generate interest and help offset some of the illustrious absentees.

It's worth noting that, in 1924, the Giro d'Italia wasn't what it is today. Bikes weighed more than eighteen kilograms, many stretches of road were unpaved and there were no gears. Still, Alfonsina threw herself into the race with gusto. And, to everyone's surprise, she completed the first seven stages, covering nearly 2,000 kilometres in the process. (By comparison, the first seven stages of the 2019 Giro covered just over half that . . . and with far better roads and equipment!) She fell repeatedly on the eighth stage, after getting caught in heavy winds and rainstorms between L'Aquila and Perugia. She still made the finish line, but, based on the rules, she should have been disqualified due to the time gap between her and the race leader. But the organisers, taken in by her spirit and determination (and perhaps cognisant that her race had captured the imagination of a nation) allowed her to continue.

She buckled down and finished the Giro, one of just thirty riders – out of the ninety who had started the race – to make it to end of the final stage in Milan. She remains the only woman to have raced in the men's Giro. And in so doing, she had kickstarted a women's cycling revolution.

'SOME OF LIFE'S GREATEST LESSONS ARE LEARNED AT THE WORST OF TIMES AND FROM THE WORST MISTAKES.'

7

THE CHRISTMAS TRUCE OF 1914

World War I began in the summer of 1914 and, despite various leaders initially saying the troops would be 'home by Christmas', by the autumn this looked increasingly unlikely. It was also clear that this war was unlike any that had hit Europe in the past – particularly for soldiers at the front.

On the one hand, it retained many of the hallmarks of the previous century, with infantrymen in hand-dug trenches, slow and ponderous troop movements and the continual scourge of disease and vermin. On the other, the killing technology had escalated to include chemical warfare, automatic fire and aerial bombardment. War is always horrific, but this one was also dirty, dreary and stressful to a degree not seen before.

Pope Benedict XV called for peace. When his words went unheeded, he asked the quarrelling nations for a Christmas truce, reminding them of the importance of the holiday during what was then an almost entirely Christian conflict. Again, few appeared to heed his plea, but some governments took notice and sent their active duty soldiers care packages.

Today, they seem almost quaint. British soldiers received a pipe, tobacco, cigarettes and a photograph of Queen Mary. Their German counterparts, in addition to the ubiquitous tobacco, received small fir trees, one for every ten infantrymen. Those fir trees would play a critical role in what happened next.

On the morning of 24 December 1914, near Ypres in Flanders (the site of one of the bloodiest battles in the early months of the war, with more than 100,000 casualties), soldiers on each side began singing Christmas carols. Several fir trees, decked out with candles and shiny ornaments, began to appear on the German trenches. The message was: 'YOU NOT SHOOT/WE NOT SHOOT'. Accounts differ of whether it was shouted or written on a sign, but the essence remained. Shortly thereafter, a lone German soldier climbed out of his trench and, arms raised, made his way into 'No-Man's Land'. Allied commanders did not know what to make of this. A few weeks earlier, a German platoon had pretended to surrender, only to lure British soldiers into an ambush, with dozens gunned down by automatic fire.

But then another German emerged, also with his arms raised, and began the slow walk towards the Allied positions. And then another. And then a fourth, and a fifth.

The Allied soldiers were dumbfounded. They stared in disbelief. Until one climbed the wooden ladder out of the trench and made his way, bare-handed, towards the Germans. And then another. And another, all in silence, bar for the occasional hymns audible through the light morning mist of a Flemish winter.

They met, they embraced, and they realised they were all young men with far more in common than they had imagined. They shared the same desire to go home and to stop being pawns in the bellicose fantasies of powerful men in government buildings. But for the accidents of their births, each could have easily been on the other side. They swapped booze for tobacco, chocolate for sausages.

This was an island of normality in the sea of insanity which Europe had become.

And then, from the English trench, a football appeared.

This was not an usual sight: it was customary to send balls into No-Man's Land as a means to signal a military manoeuvre, or the start of an artillery barrage.

But this time, the football was just that: a football.

Helmets and rucksacks formed goalposts. It may have been 11 vs 11 or 13 vs 13: nobody knows, and nobody cares. Just as the score, with hindsight, is irrelevant (although as best we can tell, the Germans won, 3–2).

The truce continued on Christmas Day and for a few days after that. But, slowly, news got back to the higher echelons of the armed forces and the government. Indeed, it made it into the newspapers too, with the *Manchester Guardian* reporting on it on New Year's Eve.

The message back to the front was swift and unambiguous: 'This is war. Fraternising with the enemy in a time of war is treason. And treason is punishable by firing squad.' The football returned to the mud and frost of the Flemish trenches. And the killing resumed. But the memory of the Christmas Truce and the possibility of a different world endured for those who had the privilege of being a part of it.

'YOU NEVER LOSE. EITHER YOU WIN OR YOU LEARN.'

8

JOHN ELWAY

By the time he was thirty-seven, John Elway had had his share of kicks in the face. And there was a monkey he could not get off his back: his position as the superstar who could not get his team over the line, the champion who excelled but fell at the final hurdle.

It's an uncomfortable position, straddling the line between winner and loser. It's especially pernicious because, in sport, the metaphysical is often cherished: the idea of having a 'strong character' and a 'winning mentality' is like some magic stardust separating the true greats from the also-rans. In Elway's case, the failures really hurt, because he had so much else going for him.

Tall and strong, he was a standout in both American football and baseball from a young age. He was good-looking, and had the intelligence to attend Stanford, one of the greatest academic universities in the US, while also competing at a high level in both his favoured sports. In his final year at Stanford, after guiding his college football team to a late lead over rival Cal (University of California, Berkley), Elway was on the receiving end of one of the most dramatic and improbable comebacks in history.

Now known simply as 'the Play', it featured no fewer than five successful lateral passes for a touchdown on a kick-off return with four seconds left. Anybody who knows even a tiny bit about American football will know how unlikely this is. Compounding the drama was the fact that the Stanford marching band, believing the game was over, had taken to the field, effectively forcing the Cal players to fight their way through them in order to reach the end zone. Elway watched powerless on the sideline as the absurdity unfolded. He would later say it would take him decades to get over 'the Play'. Many feel it cost him the Heisman Trophy as the top collegiate player in the country.

Still, Elway was chosen number one overall in the NFL draft that year. His reaction to being picked by the Baltimore Colts tells you all you need to know about his character (and why those who would later doubt him were so misguided). He announced he wouldn't play for the Colts but, instead, would pursue a career in baseball – he had the option of joining the New York Yankees – unless he was traded to a different team. Many felt he wasn't bluffing, and he got his way, ending up at the Denver Broncos.

Elway was a hit. In the late 1980s he led the Broncos to three Super Bowls in four years. His vision and fearlessness, charisma and intelligence, courage and chutzpah were unmatched. And yet he lost each of those Super Bowls. Nobody dared call him a loser in public, but there was a sense of doubt. Did he fall just short of the line between superstar and legend?

Elway himself wondered what he could do differently, what he could do better. And he knew that, with every year that passed, it would get more difficult. His body, beaten and battle-worn, couldn't do what it had done previously: not with the same effortlessness, anyway. He had to find a different path.

By 1997, he was thirty-seven years old and recovering from a ruptured biceps tendon in his throwing arm. Denver returned to the Super Bowl against the defending champions, the Green Bay Packers. He wasn't the Elway of old, and he knew it. But that game would see a critical play that would be remembered as 'the Helicopter'. It would alter the course of the game and seal Elway's place in legend.

Denver had driven deep into Green Bay territory, but it was now third down and they needed six yards. The coach called a certain formation, one which Elway didn't like. As a veteran quarterback, he had the authority to make his own decisions on the fly. Going off-script like this still took courage, but that's something Elway had plenty of. Rather than dropping back to throw, he took off right after the snap, his old legs churning the turf. As three defenders converged to tackle him, almost everyone expected him to slide, or at least stay low in order to preserve his body from a bone-jangling hit. Instead, Elway jumped in the air, attempting to take them by surprise. He was hit once, then twice, his body horizontal to the ground and swinging through the air like the blades of a chopper. He landed with a thud – and the first down. The world realised that, after so many last-ditch setbacks, this was his time. He was going to make it his time.

The Broncos won the Super Bowl – but it didn't end there. A year later, Elway returned to the Super Bowl and, once again, led the Broncos to victory. This time, with both the monkey and the pressure off his back, he dominated the game and won the Most Valuable Player award. Just to show 'the Helicopter' wasn't a fluke, he even ran for a touchdown.

'KILL THEM WITH SUCCESS, BURY THEM WITH A SMILE.'

9

DANICA PATRICK

It began the way it does with so many racing car drivers: a ride on a go-kart, usually one belonging to a friend. And suddenly, you're smitten. If you also happen to be fast – really fast – you start dreaming of how you're going to fund your passion and continue to improve.

Danica Patrick quickly fell in love with speed. And, as for talent, she had plenty. She was fearless and had a knack for choosing the right angles and making the right choices. She broke speed records at her local raceway in Wisconsin and started to attract attention, the only girl among so many boys. But there was a problem. Karting costs money and, if you're going to compete at the highest level and travel all over the country, it costs even more money. Her parents, TJ and Bev, were, like many karting parents, well-to-do enough to put their kid on the track – as long as it was local, and as long as it was only once in a while.

How were they going to fund her shot at the big time?

The same way any racer does. By creating a brand and selling it. And, at that stage – even though she thought of herself as a 'driver', not a 'girl driver' – her gender was a part of it. And so, at every race, they sold Danica merchandise: T-shirts, hats, even custom-made baseball cards. Her fame was already growing as 'the girl who beat the boys' and the merchandise ensured people remembered her. And that is exactly what sponsors want.

By the age of twelve, she had won a national kart championship. By fourteen, she had taken a 12-week course in public speaking, at her father's urging. If she was going to do this, she was going to do it right. She was already confident and charismatic and would grow into a stunningly beautiful young woman. By the time she was fifteen, MTV spent a week following her around and produced a documentary about her life and her dreams.

On the track, she continued to progress through the junior tiers of racing. She wasn't a prodigy, but she was gifted, and her fame and ability to market herself ensured she usually had access to some of the best cars and mechanics.

In 2005, she made her debut in the IndyCar series, winning her first pole in the same year. She then became the first woman to win an IndyCar race in 2008 and, in 2009, she finished third in the iconic Indianapolis 500. She later moved on to NASCAR and raced stock cars. Again, she more than held her own amidst initial scepticism. Whatever doubts people may have had about her ability on the track were, if not put to rest, at least put on hold. Even her critics had to acknowledge that she was fast. Not only that, she was brave and tough as well, taking risks and coming through crashes with the best of them.

Still, the haters hated. They pointed out that her appearance and her ability to market herself meant she attracted sponsor dollars which, in turn, meant the best teams with the best cars wanted her around. Not just that, they were more than willing to invest in her and market her once she was on board. There weren't many female race-car drivers, but there were a few – some of them more talented than her. Back in the 1970s, Janet Guthrie had become the first woman to qualify for the Indianapolis 500, yet she never enjoyed the fame, success or opportunities that Danica got. Danica, they said, only got those opportunities because of her carefully crafted image and natural beauty.

In a 2012 interview Danica addressed this head on, saying: 'Do I use being a girl to my advantage? I use everything I can to my advantage . . . maybe back in the day you didn't need to be the greatest looking to be on TV, and you didn't need to speak the best, but in this day and age, you need to be the package . . . You need to look the part for your sponsors, you need to be able to speak the part for the media.'

That honesty is not something to be taken for granted. And while you could dismiss her – as some have done – as 'the Anna Kournikova of racing', someone whose hype far exceeds her achievements, you'd be missing the point. Racing isn't just about talent. It's about playing the sponsorship game and drawing attention. And that is something Danica worked incredibly hard to do, from an early age. Perhaps more so than any other driver, male or female.

She reached her goal. She made history. And she did it her way, maximising the skills she had. All of them.

'A SIMPLE SENTENCE SPOKEN AT THE RIGHT TIME COULD CHANGE SOMEONE'S LIFE FOREVER.'

10

THE ALL BLACKS

Sometimes a sporting culture is more than just a case of a nation excelling in a particular sport. It transcends this, and becomes part of the national identity: think cricket in India, football in Brazil and ice hockey in Canada. In New Zealand, it's rugby, and it encompasses history, people, immigration and their relationship with the land itself.

The iconic All Blacks need no introduction. Their black jerseys, adorned with the silver fern, symbolise excellence in rugby and the tradition on which it is founded. The world north of the equator got to know the All Blacks way back in 1905, during a tour of the British Isles, France and the United States, during which they lost just once, to Wales. Even that match was shrouded in controversy for a try not awarded to the Kiwi winger Bob Deans.

It was also on this tour that the term 'All Blacks' entered common parlance – and it may have all been down to a typographical error. But we'll get to that.

The New Zealand rugby union had been formed just thirteen years earlier and this was their first trip to the Northern Hemisphere. They travelled by boat – via Monte-video and Tenerife – arriving in Plymouth on September 8, 1905.

They would go on to play thirty-five games over the next five months, five of them Test matches against other nations. From the very beginning, they drew a mixture of awe and curiosity: not just for the way they racked up victories, but for their approach to the game.

They were disciplined and organised to a degree few Northern Hemisphere sides had seen. They were stronger and fitter: perhaps down to the fact that, in New Zealand, matches lasted forty-five minutes, whereas in Europe at the time, they lasted just thirty-five. Most of all, once in possession, there was very little distinction between the Kiwi players. Everybody supported the attack, running and making themselves available for a pass. This was in stark contrast to 'traditional' rugby at the time, where the role of the forwards was mostly to simply win possession for the benefit of the backs. Indeed, you could say that, once in possession, New Zealand became a team of 'all-backs', where every team member was a back who could attack and demand the ball from every angle.

At least, that's how the rugby correspondent of the *Daily Mail* newspaper viewed it, after watching them destroy Huddersfield, 63–0. He wrote that they were a team of 'all-backs' but, due to a typographical error, it appeared in print as 'All-Blacks'. The name took off immediately and became their nickname in most subsequent newspaper reports. That's the origin myth of the term, and it's the one that Billy Wallace, the fullback on that New Zealand powerhouse of a touring team, told for many years afterwards. It's even in the 1966 edition of *An Encyclopaedia of New Zealand*. Who are we to argue with Wallace?

Like a lot of origin myths, it may or may not be true. Researchers who have trawled newspaper archives note that the British press initially dubbed the New Zealand team 'the Colonials', but quickly moved to All Blacks – even before the match against Hartlepool. After their very first match, the Devon-based *Express and Echo* wrote: 'The "All Blacks", as they are styled by reason of their sable and unrelieved costume . . .' But in truth, it doesn't matter. Whether the result of a misprint or simply due to the colour of their uniforms, the legend of the All Blacks was born on that tour. And 115 years later, it is stronger than ever.

'WHEN SOMEONE SAYS YOU CAN'T DO IT, DO IT TWICE AND TAKE A PICTURE.'

11

JIM ABBOTT

Necessity is the mother of invention. You probably don't need to tell Jim Abbott that. He was born without a right hand, his arm ending at the wrist. And yet, for as long as he could remember, he loved baseball and was desperate to play.

Now this is a sport which, on the surface, requires two hands, both for offence and defence. The bat is designed to be held with two hands, otherwise it's nearly impossible to generate any kind of power against pitchers who routinely hurl the ball at eighty or ninety miles per hour. And when fielding, one hand goes in the glove and the other is used for throwing. It's impossible to throw with your gloved hand and it's extremely difficult, not to mention often painful, to catch a ball bare-handed.

But Jim was determined, in the way only little boys can be. And so, his father bought him a glove and took him into the front yard to play catch, a routine rite of passage across America. It was readily apparent that Jim could throw very well, with strength and accuracy. But how was he meant to catch? Together with his dad, they figured out that he could catch the ball in his glove, secure it between his chest and forearm and, lightning quick, pull his hand out, retrieve the ball and throw it back. All in what felt like a split-second.

It worked in the yard with his dad. But could he actually

play organised baseball? Abbott was determined to find out; but first, he spent hours each day practising the glove move by himself. He'd throw the ball against a wall and catch it in his glove, perfecting his switch-and-move until it became automatic.

His coaches were sceptical at the sight of a one-handed kid wanting to play baseball. But when they saw how well he could throw, all doubt was erased from their minds. He was a special talent who threw fast and with great precision. Even if he was going to be a liability as a fielder, the reality was that most opponents would struggle to put the ball in play against such a talented pitcher.

Abbott excelled as a baseball player throughout high school. And, because he was also an exceptional athlete, he played quarterback on the football team as well. He was such a natural on the field of play that it was easy to forget that he went through a multi-step routine every time he needed to catch or field and then throw. He went on to the University of Michigan, where he played baseball, and was called up to represent the United States at the 1988 Seoul Olympics, where he duly won the gold medal.

Many of the sceptics were silenced, but not all. Abbott had the talent, and he'd found a way to overcome his physical disability on the baseball diamond at every level he encountered. But could he make it in Major League Baseball, where the hitters were that little bit better and the ball came at you that little bit faster?

He answered that question too. He was drafted out of college by the California Angels and immediately established himself as a starting pitcher. In 1991, despite the Angels finishing in last place in their division, Abbott won eighteen games and finished third in voting for the Cy Young award, the accolade for the best pitcher in the league. Two years later, pitching for the New York Yankees, he threw a complete game no-hitter, meaning that not a single batter he faced managed to get a base hit. Fewer than 250 men in nearly a century and a half of baseball had achieved the feat.

Injuries forced him to retire early a few years later, but he had made his point. One of the biographies of Abbott out there is called *Nothing to Prove*: maybe so, but he did prove plenty, above all, that when there is enough talent, desire and ingenuity, a physical disability can't stop you from reaching the pinnacle of any sport.

'IN ORDER TO BECOME THAT 1% YOU NEED TO DO WHAT 99% WON'T.'

12

EMIL ZÁTOPEK

If you're ever in Lausanne, Switzerland and visit the Olympic Park, you might come across a somewhat odd statue. It's that of a long-distance runner in mid-stride and the first thing you'll notice is probably the grimace on his face. He's in pain. A lot of pain. The other thing you'll notice is his posture, with his back held extremely straight. Nobody runs like that.

The runner depicted by the statue is Emil Zátopek, for whom suffering was a constant companion. No 'fun runs' for him.

It began when he was sixteen, working as a young apprentice in a factory that made gymnastics trainers in Prague. One day, the owner decided to organise a road race among the factory workers, gifting each of them a pair of running shoes. Emil was just an apprentice and wasn't supposed to participate, but when somebody dropped out, he figured he'd give it a go – even though the shoes were two sizes too big.

It was his first ever road race and he finished second. His fellow workers celebrated and applauded him, but Emil was angry. He wanted to win. He didn't want anybody ahead of him.

And so, he began to run in his spare time, mostly at night. His shift at the factory began at dawn and ended in the evening. No matter. A light dinner and off he went, under the flickering gaslights, through the streets of Prague.

He'd pound the streets for three, four hours. Those who encountered him, not knowing who he was, were sometimes afraid. Who was this man who looked at once desperate and disturbed? Had he escaped from an institution? Did he need help?

Head cocked, mouth open, back straight, gait asymmetrical . . . and that breathing, that very heavy breathing, as his legs hit the tarmac. It didn't seem right. His running style looked graceless and forced, which may be why, panting aside, the 'Czech Locomotive' moniker he was later given never quite suited him.

He was once asked why he ran with such desperation, such suffering marking his features, such frowns distorting his face.

'Maybe I'm not talented enough to run fast and smile at the same time,' he replied drily.

War came to Czechoslovakia and Zátopek was shipped off to the front. But he still ran, sometimes with the permission of a friendly lieutenant, sometimes in his own (rare) free time.

'If training is hard, then races are easy,' he'd tell those who asked why, after a long day on the front lines, he'd take off for a couple of hours of running. Nobody dared tell him that his next race might not be for years.

Zátopek had the power of a thoroughbred and the mentality of a mule. When he trained, he didn't just run. He'd continually speed up and slow down. Maybe without knowing it, he was the inventor of that ubiquitous 'interval training' that we now see everywhere, from local gyms to Olympic development centres.

His speciality was the 10,000 metres, a race he once won forty times in a row. Think about it. Forty consecutive 10k wins. Never a bad day. Or, to judge from his appearance, always a bad day.

He won the 10,000 metre gold at the 1948 London Olympics and, ahead of the 1952 Games in Helsinki, announced that he'd also race the 5,000 metres. The organisers tried to discourage him from competing in both races: why not give somebody else a chance? But he was determined, and so they resorted to subterfuge. They scheduled the 5,000-metre final just two days after the 10,000 metres. Surely there was no way anybody could recover in time.

Emil wasn't bothered. 'All I have to do is train harder,' he said. He'd sprint with his wife, Dana – herself an Olympic gold medallist in the javelin – perched on his shoulders. He'd do 5,000-metre runs in the snow, wearing military boots, then go and complete a 10,000-metre run.

Not only did he defend his 10,000 metre title at the 1952 Games, he set a new Olympic record. He won gold in the 5,000 metres, too, and, in so doing, set another Olympic record. Not content with that, he announced that he would also run the marathon.

He'd later say that the owner of the shoe factory, the one who had first given him the running bug, had appeared to him in a dream, telling him to do it. It seemed like a joke.

It was Zátopek's first ever marathon and nobody expected much. Nobody doubted he could finish, but a marathon is more than four times the length of the longest event in which he had ever competed. How would he pace himself? How would he know how to run?

He developed the simplest of strategies. He simply ran alongside a man named Jim Peters, the world-record holder. Zátopek figured Peters would finish near the front, so all he had to do was use him for pacing, then sprint away when they neared the finish line. Except, just before the halfway point, Zátopek realised Peters wasn't having a good day. He was slipping and, with him, so was Emil. So, he simply took off, leaving Peters behind. One by one, Zátopek raced past everybody else until he was entirely on his own. He ran straight past all the water points along the way, not realising that they were meant for the runners . . . like I said, he had never done this before.

He won, finishing a full two minutes ahead of the runner in second place. By the time Peters crossed the finish line, Zátopek had showered, changed out of his running clothes and was eating an apple.

He was a hero in Czechoslovakia, as you would expect. But he later exhibited the same bravery in politics as he did in running, and it cost him. When Soviet tanks rolled into Prague to quash the 1968 uprising, Zátopek sided with the democratic wing of the Communist party. He was stripped of his honours, humiliated and ended up working menial jobs. It wasn't until 1990, after Václav Havel's rise to power, that he was completely rehabilitated. He had won his final race as well.

'EAGLES DON'T FLY
WITH PIGEONS.'

13

JERZY KUKUCZKA

It's not about heritage and having mountains 'in your blood'. (He came from Poland, possibly the flattest country in Europe.) It's not about the equipment. (He cobbled together whatever gear he could, and on his final climb he used a rope that he had bought for a few rupees at a street market in Kathmandu.) It's not about fame and publicity. (He had very little and never sought them out.) It's not about money. (He never had any and moonlighted painting factory chimneys to pay for his trips.)

So, what is it about?

It's about the power of the mind. The idea that a young man from the town of Katowice in southern Poland can tell himself that he's going to climb the highest mountains in the world – and then go out and do it. Often on his own. Often in winter. Often by the most difficult and untested route.

There are fourteen mountains on Earth that stand 8,000 metres or taller. All of them were climbed for the very first time between 1950 and 1964. That meant that, by the time Jerzy Kukuczka was sixteen, every peak had been conquered. So, he had to find another way to stand out, another way to go – as *Star Trek* might put it – 'where no man had gone before'.

So, in 1980, when he and his friend Andrzej Czok opted to climb Mount Everest, they did it by an entirely new route, taking the South Pillar on the right-hand edge of the Southwest Face. It was a thrill: they had done something nobody else had achieved. Kukuczka vowed to do it again wherever possible, aiming not to climb in the tracks of those who had gone before, but finding his own way to the top, just as he had done on Everest.

But even that wasn't enough for him. This was the second 'eight-thousander' peak he had conquered, having climbed Lhotse the year before. Nobody had successfully climbed all fourteen of them. An Italian climber, Reinhold Messner, had already managed six. That was going to be Jerzy's challenge: to do it before Messner.

It might seem foolish, but as he stood there on top of Mount Everest, at the 'roof of the world', maybe it wasn't such a crazy idea. Perhaps you have to be in a place like that, looking out over humanity far below, to conceive of such a pursuit.

Messner had grown up in the Dolomites and had been climbing mountains his entire life. He had ascended eight-thousanders solo; and he had ascended eight-thousanders without supplemental oxygen. He was famous and well-funded and could count on state-of-the-art equipment and sponsors. He also had the knowledge and intuition that comes from being born and raised amongst the mountains. How could Jerzy hope to compete?

But, somehow, he did. Over the next five years, he climbed seven more eight-thousanders: Makalu, Broad Peak, Gasherbrum II, Gasherbrum I, Dhaulagiri, Cho Oyu and Nanga Parbat. He was up to nine. But Messner hadn't sat idle in those five years either. He had added to his total, managing another five peaks and reaching a total of twelve – only two to go for the Italian.

Maybe Jerzy knew already that Messner's lead was too great, his expertise too vast. That's why he made sure his climbs were different. All of them were done without supplemental oxygen, like Messner, but five of those seven climbs were also achieved via entirely new routes. Two others were done in winter. Winter ascents were considered foolish daredevilry by many. Not only was the weather colder, it was also far more unpredictable. The prospect of getting caught in a blizzard white-out, unable to ascend or descend, was enough to terrify most climbers. Not Jerzy.

He climbed three more eight-thousanders in 1986: Kanchenjunga, K2 and Manaslu. But by the end of that year, Messner had conquered his final two, Makalu and Lhotse. That competition was over. However, Jerzy's competition with himself continued, the ongoing feat of his mind willing his body to push beyond every limit.

A year later, he was back on the mountains, completing the very first ascent of Annapurna I in winter. A few months after that, he finished his pursuit of the world's fourteen eight-thousanders, ascending to the top of Shishapangma. Naturally, he did it 'Jerzy style'. He not only found a new route, he also lugged his skis to the top and skied down the mountain on his way back.

This brings us to his final climb, in 1989. He was attempting to ascend Lhotse via the South Face, which was previously unclimbed. The rope bearing his weight – a transport rope rather than a climbing one, and the very one that he had bought at the market – snapped, and he plunged to his death.

In some ways, it was fitting. The Cold War was ending. The Berlin Wall had fallen. A few months earlier, Lech Wałesa had been elected President of Poland, and Tadeusz Mazowiecki had become the first Polish prime minister from an Eastern Bloc nation. Jerzy's Poland – flat, poor and inward-looking, but nevertheless capable of spawning an improbable globetrotting, mountain-climbing, daredevil genius – was no more. And neither was Jerzy. But what his mind achieved against all odds – both in terms of determination and imagination – will live on in mountain lore forever.

'YOUNG PEOPLE
RUN FAST
BUT OLD PEOPLE
KNOW THE WAY.'

14

WALTER FAGNANI

Since 1973, the 100km del Passatore has been one of the world's most beautiful and breath-taking ultramarathons. It stretches from Florence, up through the hills and mountains on the border with Emilia Romagna, and back down to the finish line in Faenza. It's just above sea level at the start and finish, but climbs as high as 913 metres around halfway, at the Passo della Colla di Casaglia.

It's as taxing and physically demanding an ultramarathon as you'll find, and the fact that it unwinds among some of the most stunningly breathtaking scenery Europe has to offer adds a touch of irony. The record for the course is under six and a half hours for men and around seven and a half hours for women. But in the last few years, most of the applause has been dedicated to a man who has completed the last 45 editions of the race: Walter Fagnani. And, no, it doesn't matter that in 2019 he finished in around 19 hours.

For you see, Fagnani is ninety-four years old. And while he announced in late 2019 that he'd stop running marathons and the 'Passatore' because 'my times keep getting slower', never say never. Until he turned ninety, Fagnani would run the entire race. All one hundred kilometres of it. In the last few years, he alternated running and walking.

His fame grew as he kept competing into his eighties and, in 2015, he agreed to allow a group of researchers from the University of Verona to study him. 'You can attach whatever you want to my body, as long as it doesn't slow me down or get in my way,' he said.

He was duly strapped up with a heart rate monitor, an electrocardiogram and all sorts of other sensors relaying information in real time. He even provided a saliva sample before and after the race.

What they found was stunning. Not because it was remarkable, but because it wasn't. Everything from his oxygen consumption to his blood pressure was fully within normal parameters for a healthy man of his age. His maximum heart rate didn't go above 108 beats per minute, which is precisely what you'd expect from a fit athlete in his nineties. He didn't have a cartoonish powerful heart or massive lungs, let alone any superhero powers.

It wasn't his body that made him achieve the incredible. It was his mind. He set a goal for himself and he pursued it, without hurry, but with plenty of determination and a refusal to quit. Beyond that, there was nothing that set him apart. Yes, he had done some kind of daily physical activity ever since he was a child, but that was far from unusual for men of his generation. And, sure, by his own admission, he was an optimist: 'Sometimes, all it takes is a smile and you have an entirely different outlook on the world.' But there really was no secret: 'I go for a walk and then I have a nice glass of wine. Every single day.'

Is it that easy? How about we find out! Let's try it, and compare notes in forty years or so . . .

'IF I CHANGE THE WAY I LOOK AT THINGS, THINGS BEGIN TO CHANGE.'

15

BILLIE JEAN KING

Revolutions, especially those that bring about egalitarian change, aren't usually driven by those at the very top. Why would they push for change? The status quo generally benefits them. It takes vision to imagine a better world, courage to pursue it and, if you're already at the top of the ladder, a willingness to make sacrifices in order to see it happen.

By 1970, Billie Jean King had already won five Grand Slam singles tournaments, including three Wimbledon titles and one US Championship, as well as another eleven Grand Slam titles in singles, doubles and mixed doubles. She had held the number one ranking for three years, from 1966–8. But she was quick to realise how dysfunctional elite tennis was, despite the beginning of the Open Era two years earlier.

The Open Era had ended the practice of 'shamateurism' and ensured players could, at least, be paid as professionals. She remembered all too well advancing to the final rounds at Wimbledon while at the same time having to rely on the hundred dollars or so a week she earned teaching tennis to children in California. But while professionalism had ensured prize money and appearance fees for players, it had also sharply reinforced gender inequalities.

Prize money for men in the top tournaments was never less than three times that afforded to the women, and sometimes as high as twelve times. The argument was always the same. Men's matches drew bigger audiences, there was more interest and there were more sponsors. In fact, a number of tournament organisers dropped women's competitions altogether because they were simply less lucrative. King understood the economic argument and that it wasn't just a case of 'right vs wrong'. But at the same time, she also knew it was a self-fulfilling prophecy.

Or, to put it differently, it was a kind of closed circle. The people running the tennis tournaments generally all happened to be men. They spent more time and effort marketing the men's game, possibly because, historically, there were more male players, or possibly because they were men themselves. This marketing of the men's game drew greater audiences and, therefore, more interest from media and sponsors, which equated to more money flowing to the men. And because they generated more money, they were marketed more heavily. And on it went.

There was one way to break this circle, she thought: go it alone. She teamed up with her then-husband, Larry King, as well as Gladys Heldman – a former pro, tireless advocate for the women's game and publisher of *World Tennis* magazine – to create a new tournament circuit, one devoted exclusively to women's tennis. They were joined by eight other top players and held their first event in Houston. They secured a major sponsor, Virginia Slims, signed guaranteed contracts for the princely sum of one dollar (plus a share of profits, taking a leap of faith that there would, in fact, be profits one day) and off they went.

It wasn't charity. Nor was it just a battle for social justice. It came from a belief that having a dedicated tour with dedicated marketing and publicity efforts could grow the women's game. And, economically, they were vindicated. These days, tennis is probably the major sport where gender inequality is lowest, whether in terms of coverage, sponsorship or revenue. For women athletes everywhere, not just tennis, it was a hugely empowering move.

And it came at a personal cost. Many women pros were reluctant to join what they considered to be a 'rebel organization' particularly once the United States Lawn Tennis Association, the sport's governing body in the US, suspended those women who joined the Virginia Slims Circuit. In some cases, they were pressured not to join it by their (usually male) coaches, agents or family members. Acrimony grew, relationships were damaged. But within a few years, the Virginia Slims Circuit had absorbed the 'official' women's tours. In 1973, it became a global organisation as Billie Jean King became a founding member of the Women's Tennis Association.

That may have been, in practical terms, the main turning point in driving gender equality in sports. In terms of publicity however, King soon found herself at the centre of another event, one which was just as important: the 1973 'Battle of the Sexes', pitting her against Bobby Riggs.

Riggs had won Wimbledon in 1939 and was a former world number one. Now in his mid-fifties, he travelled the US as a sort of showman/hustler, playing exhibitions and drawing huge crowds. He was a master self-promoter who relentlessly appeared across the media, mocking the women's game and insisting that, even in his fifties, he could easily beat any top woman. Because of the formation of the Virginia Slims Circuit and King's advocacy of equal prize money, she was an easy target and he taunted relentlessly, challenging her to a match. King declined, not wishing to be part of Riggs' act, but Margaret Court, the world number one, accepted. Riggs duly beat her 6–2, 6–1 and milked it as much as he could. He appeared on the covers of both *Sports Illustrated* and *Time* magazine and revelled in his chauvinism. Many casual observers came to the conclusion that maybe Riggs was right: maybe women's tennis was so inferior that it deserved neither comparable prize money nor much attention.

Riggs challenged King again, and this time she felt she needed to accept. The match drew enormous audiences – estimated at some 90 million worldwide – and was played at the hulking Astrodome in Houston. King knew she had to win; she knew what the stakes were. And she changed her game as a result, in order to take advantage of the twenty-six year age gap. Rather than playing her usual aggressive game, she was patient, forcing Riggs to cover the whole court, eventually tiring himself out. She won 6–4, 6–3, 6–3.

What was intended by Riggs as a publicity stunt took on a far greater significance in the minds of many. Perhaps one that, in terms of how we perceive the women's game, was just as critical as King's decision to take a leap into the unknown and form her 'by women, for women' rebel tour.

'A GOOD TEACHER
IS LIKE A CANDLE.
IT CONSUMES ITSELF
TO LIGHT THE WAY
FOR OTHERS.'

16

JOCH STEIN

Jock Stein never lacked a sense of place and roots. It couldn't have been any other way. He went 'down the pits' – working in the coalmines of Lanarkshire – as a teenager, combining his work as a miner with his football career, which, initially, was as an amateur at Albion Rovers. This was, in part, because he was seventeen when World War II broke out and, while footballers could get called up to fight, mining was considered a 'reserved occupation' meaning miners were so important to the war effort, they were spared the call to arms.

It wasn't until after the war that Stein turned professional, albeit in the Welsh Football League, before returning to what would become his spiritual home: Celtic. He was twenty-seven and was picked up as a reserve team player, but his personality, leadership skills and empathy soon made him stand out, and he captained the team that won the 1953–54 Double, winning both the Scottish League and the Cup. The club were so grateful that they paid for every player to attend the 1954 World Cup in Switzerland. Stein's eyes were opened to a much wider world, one that he had known was out there but had never imagined he would be a part of.

But if the seed for a future in management was planted here, so too was another realisation: that identity matters. The success of the teams he saw on the pitch wasn't merely down to superior talent or athleticism: there was a common culture, a unifying sense of purpose and an idea of who they were.

That stuck with him even as, a few years later, he moved into management, rising through the ranks and returning to Celtic in 1965, becoming the club's first-ever Protestant manager (and only the fourth in its entire almost-eighty-year history). Stein began to shape the team, helping legendary players like Billy McNeill and Jimmy Johnstone come into their own.

That December, he made a trip to Naples which underscored the humility and attention to detail that would make him one of the greatest managers ever. Scotland were playing Italy in a World Cup qualifier. Stein was only there to watch the game, but when he spotted the Italian fullback Giacinto Facchetti in the hotel lobby, he seized the opportunity. Facchetti had starred in the Inter side that had won two consecutive European Cups under Helenio Herrera. Inter played a style of football that befuddled opponents, based on staunch defending and lightning-quick counter-attacks.

Stein, accompanied by an interpreter, approached Facchetti and congratulated him on Inter's success. He then charmed him into a long conversation, during which he extracted as much information as he could about the way Inter played. Facchetti was only too happy to share.

As fate would have it, eighteen months later, Inter faced Celtic in the final of the European Cup. Stein's fact-finding mission would prove invaluable. But, just as important, if not more, was his team. That Celtic side already had an aura of invincibility, having won every competition they had entered that year. Crucially, they had a sense of identity: every single one of the players who started in that 1967 European Cup final in Lisbon was born within twenty-five miles of Glasgow. Every last one. They shared a sporting culture but, thanks to Stein, also had the humility to learn from others outside that culture.

Perhaps that's why they were entirely unfazed when Inter took the lead after just seven minutes. On the surface, the game was ideally placed for the Italian team to sit back, soak up pressure and hit on the counterattack. In reality, because Stein had figured out how Inter tended to counter, Celtic could neutralise most of their moves. He had also changed the narrative, giving his men the sense that if the two-time European champions were defending so deep, it was because they were desperate. And that's how it played out. Celtic peppered Inter's goal with a staggering 39 shots. Eventually they broke through with Tommy Gemmell and Stevie Chalmers, and secured their place in history, becoming the first club from the British Isles to win the European Cup.

The fact that Stein did it entirely with local players – a feat that will almost certainly never be matched – made his figure immortal, even though he would pass away after suffering a heart attack at just sixty-two years of age. By that point, he was manager of Scotland, and it happened pitch-side, during a World Cup qualifier against Wales. Stein had given his all to passing on his twin messages of roots and humility, lighting the way for others – including his then-assistant, the future Sir Alex Ferguson – to follow. Perhaps that's why, as legend has it, his final words were: 'I'm feeling much better now.'

'DON'T BE SO HARD
ON YOURSELF.'

17

TAZIO NUVOLARI

They call it 'drifting'. You may know it from *The Fast and the Furious: Tokyo Drift*. It's basically a controlled skid around a corner, where you turn your front wheels sharply before a bend and allow the car to understeer its way around it.

It's terrifying.

It must have been even scarier in the days of Tazio Nuvolari, racing open-cockpit cars around the dusty roads of 1930s Europe.

It also explains why the legendary racer went through dozens of co-pilots during his career: few could stomach being in the cockpit with him.

Nuvolari was slight of build and olive-skinned, with narrow-set eyes that would spark into life as if lit by touch-paper. He drove in the Italian army during World War I and was soon given an ambulance to ferry the sick and wounded. One day a general hitched a ride, sitting alongside him. Nuvolari drove his way – which meant white knuckles, raised hair and terror at every turn – and ended up spinning off the road.

The general, none too amused, looked at him.

'This is the last time you're getting behind the wheel, son,' he told Nuvolari. 'You'll still be transporting the wounded; you'll just be carrying them on stretchers. At least that way you won't be going as fast and you'll do less damage. Evidently, driving is not something you know how to do . . .' Famous last words and all that.

Was he discouraged? Was he heck!

In 1920, two years after the war ended, Nuvolari was back behind the wheel, this time racing for real. First motorbikes, then automobiles . . . it mattered little. He always raced wearing the outfit that would become his trademark: yellow shirt, black leather jacket, sky-blue trousers and a tricolour ribbon around his neck.

His approach to racing was a dangerous cocktail of need for speed and obliviousness to danger. Safety was not the point.

In 1925, Alfa Romeo's engineers proudly completed a new version of their new P2 model and invited him to test it at Monza.

'Tazio, we think this is the most powerful engine yet, but we haven't yet tested the car at high speeds,' they told him. 'Please take it easy; we don't know how it's going to react.' 'Well, somebody has to find out, right?' Nuvolari replied, as he stepped into the vehicle.

Minutes later he had crashed out after flooring the accelerator and pushing the car beyond its limits. He was taken to hospital with multiple fractures.

To many, it was a disaster. In six days' time, he was scheduled to race in the Gran Premio delle Nazioni, the premier motorcycle competition of its time. Sponsors had paid handsomely to have him there and tickets had been sold on the back of his growing popularity. And here he was, with limbs in plaster casts on a hospital bed.

Logic and self-preservation suggested he'd be a no-show.

Instead, he was wheeled to the start line on a gurney as the crowd murmured among themselves in hushed tones. With casts and bandages everywhere, Nuvolari was tightly strapped into a racing position. Three men picked him up and put him on the bike, bandages flapping in the light breeze.

He won, of course, because that's what he did. But not without drama. He might have been faster than everyone, but the lack of mobility under his casts and bandages caused him to scrape against the wall of the track, breaking two bones in his hand. One of the bones would cut clean through his racing glove, sticking out and flashing red as he sped by, like a hazard sign on a dashboard.

Broken limbs would become a regular feature of his triumphs. In 1934, he won the German Grand Prix less than six weeks after breaking his right leg in multiple places. He had no feeling in his right foot, so he asked the mechanics to change the pedals and drove entirely with his left.

He was determined to win, by any means necessary. In Turin in 1946, he gripped the steering wheel so hard that he broke it, pulling it clean out of the cockpit. No matter. A quick pit stop, and he figured he could shove an adjustable wrench in its place and steer that way. He didn't win – jury-rigging the steering cost him too much time – but he still finished, and gave the leaders a scare into the bargain.

Plenty of people offered pop psychological assessments of his recklessness. Was he simply an adrenaline junkie or was there something else, something darker, behind his apparent disregard for his own life and wellbeing?

Nuvolari himself said several times that dying on the racetrack would be a way to once again be with his sons, Giorgio and Alberto, both of whom had died as teenagers: the former of myocarditis, the latter of meningitis. But as an explanation it doesn't quite stack up: he was already 45 when Giorgio passed, and 54 when Alberto died. By that point, he'd been racing and putting his life on the line in daredevil fashion for more than two decades.

More ominously, perhaps, this was a man who stayed alive by challenging death, daring death to take him. After developing a serious, incurable chronic pulmonary infection, he continued racing undeterred, although he now had to race left-handed – using his right to grip the handkerchief that wiped the blood he'd cough up. He often still won, as he did at the Albi Grand Prix in 1946.

'Death is the true soulmate of every motor racer,' he said in one of his final interviews. 'I tried to seduce her a thousand times on the track. But she never wanted me, I guess. I am destined to die in my own bed.' And so, it came to pass. A combination of his infected lungs, a stroke that caused him to be partially paralysed and a second one that left him bed-ridden meant that Nuvolari could race no more. In 1953, he was buried under the inscription: 'You will race even faster along the roads of Heaven.'

'A GOAL WITHOUT A PLAN IS JUST A WISH.'

18

NATALIE DU TOIT

It was a Monday morning and, like she did most mornings, Natalie Du Toit trained before school. She hopped on her scooter afterwards, as she always did, and made her way through Newlands, the leafy suburb at the foot of Table Mountain near Cape Town. What happened next changed her life.

She was hit by a car and knocked off her scooter, breaking her leg in four places. It was as nasty a freak accident as doctors had seen. And when, even after two operations, it showed no signs of healing, the medical team told her they'd have to amputate her leg.

Natalie took the news the way she took most news: with a shrug and a grin, more interested in calming down those around her than what it meant for her own life. And it meant a lot. Ever since she had been a little girl, she had devoted herself to swimming. Three years earlier, when she was fourteen, she had qualified for the 1998 Commonwealth Games in Kuala Lumpur, representing South Africa. She dreamed of the 2004 Athens Olympics. Not just of being there, mind you, but of winning a medal.

And now? Her coach, Karoly von Toros, had little doubt: 'One days she will make it to the Olympics.' Natalie, naturally, agreed.

Less than three months later, before she was even fitted with the prosthetic leg that would allow her to walk again, Natalie was back in the pool, churning out the laps. The Commonwealth Games were the following year in Manchester, and she planned on being there. Despite still adjusting to her disability, she set world records in her Paralympic races, but she also made sporting history by qualifying for the able-bodied 800-metre final. It was the first time that an athlete with a disability had qualified for the final of a major able-bodied event.

Natalie dominated Paralympic swimming and pushed on, determined to replicate her achievement in able-bodied events as well. But then it struck her: competing with one fewer limb against athletes who, like her, had spent their entire lives in swimming pools was maybe too much of a mountain to climb. You can't lose twenty-five per cent of your forward propulsion and hope to keep up, not against swimmers as talented and as hard-working as she was.

So, she figured she'd level the playing field, so to speak. Open-water swimming was going to be an Olympic event in Beijing in 2008. It would be the first time since the very first modern Olympics back in 1896 that events would be held in open waters. While it had grown in popularity in recent years as a leisure pursuit, competitive open-water swimming was still relatively new, with the first world events only held in the 1990s.

Swimmers were still figuring out the best way to compete against the challenges it presented. There were currents and waves to deal with, and waters that could be choppy. A sense of direction was critical as, with no reference points other than the occasional buoy, it was easy to go off course.

Natalie was convinced she could figure all this out. And she knew she wouldn't be competing against the very best swimmers in the world, tucked away in the reassuring familiarity of identical, perfectly kept pools, but rather with free spirits, those willing to push themselves and test themselves in the open water. This was a game-changer. Even without a leg, she felt she could compete.

She'd still have to learn an entirely new way of swimming, as well as figuring out currents and waves, working out how to get her sense of direction right and, of course, improving her stamina. Open-water races can be ten kilometres long, nearly seven times as long as the longest pool races.

But, in her confident, carefree way, Natalie figured she had plenty of time on her hands to build her stamina. And off she went.

Natalie didn't just compete. She finished fourth at the Open Water World Championships in Seville, enabling her to qualify for Beijing. And in the Chinese capital, up against women with far more experience in the open water and fully able-bodied, she finished sixteenth in a field of twenty-five.

We often think of athletes' bodies as perfectly balanced machines. When a cog fails, or is no longer there, we expect them to fall apart. That may be true. But when you have the mind and the attitude of someone like Natalie Du Toit, even a missing leg is something you can overcome, if you're clever enough – and patient enough – in how you readjust and reposition yourself.

'YOUR CHILD FOLLOWS YOUR EXAMPLE NOT YOUR ADVICE.'

19

GIACOMO SINTINI

Giacomo 'Jack' Sintini was on top of the world. He was an Italian international volleyball player and a European champion, having choreographed Italy's 2005 European Volleyball Championship win, which ended with a dramatic tie-break victory over Russia in the final. He had a wife who he adored, Alessia, and a daughter over whom he fussed, Carolina. It was 2010 and he was thinking ahead to the 2012 Olympics.

'Then, one night, I went to bed after a game feeling a little tired but otherwise great. I woke up the next morning with a severe pain in my upper back, right beneath my shoulder blade,' he recounts.

This was in late spring. Sintini gritted his teeth and played out the rest of the season thinking it might simply be a case of overexertion. Volleyball makes your body move in strange, sometimes unnatural ways. A lifetime on the court might have caught up with him.

He tried painkillers, he tried absolute rest, he tried whatever the doctors suggested. But nothing worked. That area of the body is tricky to diagnose anyway, but in this case, they were particularly nonplussed. 'Swimming can't hurt,' they told him, 'as long as you don't overdo it. It will loosen up the muscles and give you some flexibility. See if that helps,' they insisted.

But one day, while swimming lengths, just as his hand

hit the end of the lane, Sintini felt the strongest, most violent pain he had ever experienced. It was so strong, it felt as if it was pulling him down, towards the bottom of the pool. He nearly drowned that day.

'I was terrified that it was something that might cost my career,' he said. 'As it turned out, it was far worse. It was something that could have cost me far more.'

He received his diagnosis on 1 June. He had stage four non-Hodgkin lymphoma. It was spreading throughout the inside of his body. Two ribs were effectively pulverised by this stage, and most of his internal organs were severely affected.

He was immediately put on a hardcore regimen of medication and chemotherapy. And when that didn't work, the doctors doubled down, ratcheting up the dose. In a few months he lost twenty-three kilograms from his six-feet, five-inch frame. He was tempted to let go, to give up, to let nature run its course and the Almighty decide his fate.

'But then I thought about my little girl,' he said. 'And I realised I never wanted her to grow up thinking her father was somebody who would just throw in the towel and surrender.'

The doctors come up with one final solution, an autologous bone marrow transplant. It was painful and laborious, and the possibility of success at this stage was minimal. But even as he returned from hospital after the surgery, not knowing what effect, if any, it would have, Jack felt better. Why? Because he was fighting back. Because he was reacting. Because he was not passive. Maybe it was all in his head. But he felt strangely empowered.

And in the next few months, the cancer receded. The therapy worked. Jack felt himself getting stronger. He went back to the gym, to the volleyball court. A few sets, a few spikes, just for fun. And on 8 May 2012, less than a year after that terrible diagnosis, he was given the medical all-clear. He could play again, if he so chose.

It was obviously too late for London 2012. But simply knowing he could play again, that he had beaten cancer, was worth it. He didn't expect to return to the court at the highest level, not now that his scrawny sixty-eight kilograms were spread over his tall, gaunt frame. He still looked more like a skeleton than an athlete. But he got a call from a team in Trentino, in the northeast of Italy. They were looking for a reserve setter to back up the Brazilian Raphael, one of the best in the world at his position. Would he consider it?

Jack jumped at the chance. He knew he wouldn't play much, but it would be enough simply to be able to train and be part of a team. It was now eighteen months since his last competitive match. He joined Trentino and things turned out largely as expected. He worked extremely hard, but very rarely got on the court. Raphael was just too good; the team couldn't afford not to have him play. And, truth be told, Jack was still a shadow of his former self – and having now turned thirty-four, it was not likely he would improve much.

But then the story took a twist. Trentino reached the final of the Italian league championship, where they faced Piacenza in a 'best of five' series. And after four games, with the score deadlocked at 2–2, Raphael fractured his finger. The coach had no choice but to send on Jack to replace him.

And just like in a Hollywood film, there's a Hollywood ending. Jack started the fifth and final game and directed traffic beautifully for Trentino. Any concerns that he couldn't hold up physically were washed away. That he'd have the mental fortitude to do it was never in question: after all, he had beaten cancer. There's pressure – and then there's real pressure. That day, 12 May 2013, Jack not only led Trentino to the title, he was also voted Most Valuable Player.

He said it was the most beautiful day of his life. Maybe because he proved to his little girl that not only does Daddy never give up, he's strong enough to come back and achieve the unthinkable.

'BE WHO YOU WANT TO BE.'

20

RONDA ROUSEY

Ronda Rousey faced more adversity before she was ten than most face in a lifetime. She was born with her umbilical cord wrapped around her neck, causing a speech disorder that meant she could not form an intelligible sentence until she was six, after years of speech therapy. While taking his three daughters sledding, her father, Ronald, broke his back. Later, after the degenerative damage to his spine caused him to become a paraplegic, he took his own life. Ronda was eight at the time.

If you think these experiences might have made her tough and unemotional, you're only half-right. She's tough, sure. But she's anything but unemotional. She cries frequently, laughs frequently and won't even consider answering questions about the loss of her father, because she feels 'it would be prostituting his memory'.

The origins of the toughness that made her the most famous female Mixed Martial Artist – heck, for a while, the most famous MMA star, regardless of gender – may be debatable, but her mother was a big part of it. AnnMaria De Mars was a black belt in judo who won the 1984 world championships, training Ronda from the age of eleven. Ronda would go on to follow in her mother's footsteps, winning bronze in judo at the 2008 Olympics in Beijing.

Those around her expected Ronda to buckle down and begin training for London 2012. She had been one of the youngest judokas in the field in Beijing and would just be entering her prime at the next Olympics. But Rousey wasn't sure about making four years of sacrifices for, as she put it, 'ten grand and a handshake'. She considered going to university, although she wasn't sure about simply settling into everyday civilian life either.

And so, she opted for MMA. It was neither an obvious choice, nor a safe one. Yes, she was strong and powerful and a judo champion. But judo outfits are designed to be loose, offering plenty of strong fabric for judokas to grab on to. In MMA, you wear singlets, making the sort of throws and grips which are judo staples nearly impossible. Second, a big part of MMA involves punching and kicking, something which would have been entirely new to her, both in terms of dishing them out as well as absorbing them.

And, finally, judo had established tournaments and a circuit for men and women. MMA was growing rapidly in terms of men's competition, but the women's circuit was still a bit of a novelty. In fact, Dana White's Ultimate Fighting Championship (UFC), the leading promotion in the sport, didn't have a women's division. White himself would later explain that he wasn't sure it was commercially viable. There were a handful of gifted women fighters, but they were often seen as very masculine and uncharismatic. They didn't appeal to MMA audiences that, at the time, were overwhelmingly male. And, indeed, they didn't appeal to the small audience of women who followed MMA either. More feminine fighters didn't come across as tough enough. MMA audiences – regardless of their own gender – were purists. They weren't interested in what you might term as 'eye candy'. At least, that was the conventional wisdom of the time, however sexist and prejudiced it might appear today.

Rousey was undeterred. She would give it a shot. She began training, mostly with men, supporting herself by waitressing and bartending. She moved into MMA in 2010 and turned pro a year later. She was an instant hit, not just for her success – her fights were usually over quickly, either through her trademark armbar and submission, or because her flurry of punches knocked out opponents – but also because purist (male) MMA fans gave her respect very quickly. Her technical ability was evident, but equally she had the femininity of a woman. Not a delicate flower of a woman, but a very strong, athletic woman.

Her popularity and ability to appeal to both men and women in a physical, punishing sport persuaded White to launch a women's division in UFC. And, for Rousey, that moved the needle, both financially and in terms of fame. She was one of the first MMA fighters to truly cross-over into mainstream consciousness and was arguably as famous as any male UFC star.

After six successful title defences, she lost her belt to Holly Holm in November 2015 and fell again, to Amanda Nunes, a year later. But it didn't matter: her contribution to the sport was sealed. She moved into acting and later signed with World Wrestling Entertainment (WWE).

And while she faced plenty of pressure to return to the octagon, she had come to terms with what she'd achieved and who she was.

'It's hard . . . [when the thing people value about you] is how you fight,' she would say. 'And how they see you is how you fight, and the only thing they think you have to offer is how you fight . . . [but] I'm so much more than just a fighter.'

Indeed, she was a trailblazer who put a sport on the map, while also creating a new paradigm for women athletes. And if she ever does return to the octagon, it will be on her own terms.

'THE PAIN YOU
FEEL TODAY WILL BE
THE STRENGTH YOU'LL
FEEL TOMORROW.'

21

VINNY PAZIENZA

Vinny Pazienza was fortunate. At five years of age, he knew what he wanted to be when he grew up: a fighter, like Muhammad Ali. But Paz, as everybody called him (so much so that he would later legally change his name), lacked the natural grace and athleticism of Ali. What he did have, in industrial quantities, was grit and toughness.

When, at age fourteen, he watched *Rocky* in the cinema, he knew that this was his journey too. Rocky could outlast and outwork the opposition, and so would he. Pazienza turned professional at age 21, in 1983, having laid waste to the amateur ranks not just in his native Rhode Island, but up and down the Atlantic coast. His father bought a derelict fire station for $17,500 and turned it into a gym, appropriately called 'Fathers and Sons'. They were 'all in'.

Four years later, Pazienza became world champion for the first time, winning the International Boxing Federation (IBO) lightweight belt. But there was a problem: Pazienza was not a natural lightweight. Before every match, he subjected himself to diets and saunas. This gained him some speed, sure – hence the moniker that would accompany him throughout his career, 'Pazmanian Devil' – but he lost power.

He moved up to light welterweight and, on three occasions, fought for the world title, losing each time. He put his body through the most extreme of punishments. In

1988, he lost a prize fight to Roger Mayweather, just 34 days after his last fight. In another title fight, in 1990, Loreto Garza turned his face into a bloodied mess before Pazienza went 'full devil' on him, attempting to body slam him and promptly getting disqualified.

That fight marked a sea change. Pazienza disappeared for eight months and returned as middleweight. He became only the second boxer ever to become world champion at both lightweight and middleweight: that was in 1991, when he overcame Gilbert Dele.

Less than a month later, he was driving near his home in Cranston when he was hit head-on by a truck. He woke in hospital with two broken vertebrae in his neck and tearful doctors telling him he would probably never walk again. As for fighting, that would be out of the question.

But Pazienza willed himself better. Within a week, he was taking his first tentative steps around his hospital room. Shortly thereafter he was released, albeit wearing a medical device called a 'halo': a circular metal brace that screwed into his skull in four spots and was propped up with four metal rods resting on his shoulders.

Less than a week after having his halo brace fitted – and, obviously, against doctors' orders – he resumed his workout regime, sneaking into his basement weight room. He hit the iron hard, pumping away and pushing his broken body, without telling anyone.

'I never believed anything doctors told me,' he would later say. 'It never occurred to me that I would never fight again. When I closed my eyes, I could already see and hear the crowd cheering me on in the ring.' He wore the halo brace for three months. With hindsight, it's a miracle he did not injure himself further by working out in those circumstances, especially as the contraption was effectively an additional 11 kilograms resting on his shoulders and his head.

When the time came to remove the halo brace, his

doctors offered him a total anaesthetic, as you would expect. Pazienza bluntly refused.

'Pain is a wonderful teacher,' he told them. 'And I want to learn to suffer more.' As they took the screws out of his head, the pain was so severe that he reacted by ripping the armrest off the wooden chair on which he was seated. Still, the pain taught him.

With the halo gone, he was back in the ring. But he had a problem. Nobody wanted to fight him, or even spar with him. Everyone knew what he had been through, and everyone was terrified of hurting him.

It took a while, but on 15 December 1992, he was back in the ring, defeating Luis Santana. It was Pazienza who was dishing out the hurt. A year after that, he was a world champion again, knocking out Dan Sherry for the IBO super middleweight title.

But the very cream of the crop still avoided him, at least until, at the iconic MGM Grand Garden Arena in Las Vegas, he took on the legendary Roberto Durán, the man with 'hands of stone'. Durán was twelve years his senior and a veritable giant of boxing. The match quickly turned into a brawl, and Pazienza's face into a beaten-up mess resembling butcher's scraps. But Pazienza danced and twirled and hit and refused to go down. By the end, the judges' scorecards were clear: he had won, no matter how bruised and bloodied.

Durán was furious, and Pazienza immediately agreed to a rematch. Six months later, Pazienza won again, retaining the title. That second Durán match is remembered for Pazienza taking blow after blow as if to say 'Is that all you got? You can't hurt me!'

A frustrated Durán eventually succumbed, although, afterwards, Pazienza would reveal: 'Those blows did hurt. Each punch was like a wrecking ball exploding into my face. But the pain only made me stronger . . .' And in his case, it did.

'YOU GET TO DECIDE THE LEGACY THAT YOU LEAVE.'

22

STANLEY MATTHEWS

When Sir Stanley Matthews made his debut for Stoke City, Adolf Hitler and the Nazis had not yet come to power in Germany. When he played his final match as a professional, Alexei Leonov was on the verge of completing the first spacewalk in the history of humanity.

That ought to provide some scale to the career of a man who became a byword for persistence and longevity. He played for two clubs in his career: Stoke City, his hometown team (although apparently he was a fan of their bitter rivals, Port Vale) and Blackpool. The fact that neither was a genuine powerhouse helps explain why his trophy cupboard was relatively bare: just the one FA Cup in 1953.

He had a sense of loyalty, discipline and routine during his playing days, which was at once at the heart of his success and also the reason that he didn't win more silverware. At a time when most English footballers were *bon vivants* he was neither particularly gregarious nor sociable, opting instead for an almost monkish lifestyle (by the standards of the day). He very rarely drank alcohol, he avoided cigarettes (although he was happy to advertise them for a fee), and he ate a diet rich in fruit and vegetables at a time when many thought red meat was the key to an athlete's success. He supplemented club training with sessions on his own, often running on sand or wearing specially made heavy boots, so he'd feel lighter on his feet when wearing normal shoes.

His father had been a boxer and he very nearly went down that route. But whatever toughness he inherited was channelled towards a rigid self-discipline. He started his career centrally and soon moved to the wing, establishing himself as the 'wizard of the dribble'. He had lightning-fast feet that allowed him to take more touches in tight spaces, the key to beating many opponents, but he also had the ability to just knock the ball past them and take off down the wings. Football was often a series of individual battles in those years, and if you could beat a man and create an overload, you were well on your way to success.

That's how, in 1953, Matthews came to dominate the biggest game in English club football, the FA Cup Final, in a match which is now remembered as the 'Matthews Final'. The game itself took on an outsized importance in the history of English football for reasons that had nothing to do with him: televised sport was in its infancy, and many Britons had bought or rented sets for the imminent coronation of Queen Elizabeth II and so were able to watch the match.

An hour into the game, Blackpool found themselves 3–1 down against the Bolton Wanderers. Matthews, who had already set up Blackpool's opening goal with a brilliant cross for Stan Mortensen, took over. He provided the final pass for two of the three further goals Blackpool would score, to eventually win 4–3. More than that, if you watch the highlights – available on YouTube – you will see just how much impact he had on the game. Every time the ball came to him in his familiar right-wing position, a sense of panic seemed to envelop the opposition. Typically, he'd set off, shoulder hunched, ball at his feet, twisting one way and the other, then suddenly accelerating into space before delivering a cross. You got the sense that every one of those dribbling moves had been practised a million times by Matthews, probably on his own – and probably on his own time. Nothing was casual or coincidental.

The fact that he was thirty-eight at the time – in an era when most players retired in their early thirties – makes it all the more remarkable. You would never guess he was that old from watching the footage. And you certainly wouldn't guess that he would go on to play for another twelve seasons, retiring a few days after his fiftieth birthday. His record stood until it was broken in 2017 by Japanese striker Kazuyoshi Miura.

His set of tricks and feints on the wing had become so ingrained, and his fitness so good for a man of his age, that he continued playing for the English national side as well. Indeed, when he played for England for the final time in 1957, he was forty-two years old: the oldest player to ever represent the country. Over an international career that spanned twenty-three seasons, he won fifty-four caps. And the total would certainly have been higher if, for six years during the prime of his career – from the ages of twenty-four to thirty – football hadn't effectively been suspended in England due to the war.

Upon retirement, Matthews maintained his rigorous diet and exercise regime for as long as he could. And he put his football fame to good use, coaching youngsters around the world well into his early seventies. He showed, too, that he was unafraid to ruffle political feathers, when in 1975 when he broke apartheid rules in South Africa to set up a team in the black township of Soweto. But that was Matthews. He marched to the beat of his own drummer, always on the rigorous straight and narrow. And he did it for a long time – longer than anyone else.

'ONE DAY ALL YOUR HARD WORK WILL PAY OFF.'

23

PIETRO MENNEA

The year was 1980 and Pietro Mennea was heading for his third Olympic games. In 1972 in Munich he had won bronze in the 200 metres; four years later, in Montreal, he had just missed out on a medal, finishing fourth. His times told you he was one of the best sprinters around. In 1979, he managed a personal best of 10.01 in the 100-metre dash and a world record 19.72 in the 200 metres, a mark that would stand for nearly seventeen years, until Michael Johnson clocked 19.66 at the US Olympic Trials in 1996.

But here's the thing. Mennea wasn't the fastest. He was a guy who sprinted very well. There's a difference, and it was most evident in the 200 metres, his speciality. It was also why he was much better over that distance than over 100 metres. The latter is a pure, flat-out, straight-line sprint. Whatever thinking is involved lies in your reaction time to the starter's gun and the focus your mind can put on your limbs moving as quickly as they can. For ten seconds or so, there is nothing for your brain to do other than to metaphorically mercilessly whip the body into going as hard as it can.

It's not that running the 100 metres doesn't require technique or application. It certainly does. You can gain efficiencies and make yourself faster by teaching yourself the right form in order to maximise the power in every stride and minimise things like drag and wind resistance.

But all of that happens before the race, in training. Once you get down into those blocks, the difference between winning and losing is essentially down to three things: your reaction time at the start, the muscle memory you accumulated in training that helps you unconsciously maintain the perfect form and, of course, how much power and speed your muscles can generate. That's all it is, really.

But the 200-metre dash is a different race, owing to that one big curve in the middle of it. It's not a race you can run with your eyes closed. At some point you need to angle your run. You have to do it at the right time, choose the right trajectory to ensure that not an ounce of your energy is wasted. That's where Mennea excelled: in capturing the split second. Raw speed and power? Not compared to his fellow world-class sprinters. Brilliant technique? Not at all – compared to others, he looked more awkward than fluid. The edge was in his head. Where he really had blazing speed was in the velocity of his thought.

Back to Moscow. It was a strange Olympics for Mennea personally, and for the wider world too. Mennea had not run particularly well in the year leading up to the Games and, in fact, had struggled to get the necessary qualifying times to even go. Still, ahead of the competition, he was seen as the favourite, since the United States-led boycott had cleared the field of some of his fiercest competitors.

That said, the reigning Olympic champion, Jamaica's Don Quarrie, was in the final, as was the English sprinter Allan Wells. And Mennea was also given position number eight, the far outside lane, in the draw for starting positions. These days, lane assignments are based on seeding and lane eight goes to the bottom seed. Why? Because you have the lowest amount of centripetal force when you come out of the curve and on to the straight. Psychologically it's also sub-optimal, because your starting point is well ahead of the others, meaning you can't see any of your opponents until the end of the curve. Tiny margins, tiny differences, of course, but in a race of twenty seconds or so, every split second matters.

Mennea knew he needed to run the perfect race to have a prayer. And when the race began, it looked as if everything was going to go wrong. Wells, just to the inside of him in lane seven, burst out of the blocks and, twenty metres in, had already passed Mennea. As the end of the curve approached, Mennea was sixth. But he burst out of the curve and on to the straight like a missile out of a slingshot, accelerating towards the gold in one of the most dramatic finishes in Olympic sprint history.

His legs, lungs and muscles had carried him to Olympic gold. But it was his mind that had brought it all together, choosing the perfect path around the curve and on to the straight, and giving him the momentum to burn his way to the finish, just milliseconds ahead of Wells.

'NOAH LOOKED LIKE A FOOL UNTIL IT STARTED TO RAIN. KEEP BUILDING.'

24

COLIN CHAPMAN

If you want to compete, you can either do what everybody else does and hope to do it better, or you can do things differently. Colin Chapman was one of those rare men who chose the latter option. A natural non-conformist, right down to his trademark black cap, he was a brilliant engineer who made it into Formula One by avoiding the groupthink that so often befell his rivals (and which he loved to ridicule).

His greatest intuition came in the spring of 1976, and it was an example of a brilliant mind interpreting an unexpected event differently to everyone else. He was chief engineer at Lotus at the time and conducting tests in the wind tunnel in preparation for designing the following year's model. Wind tunnel modelling is usually done with a chassis made primarily of plywood that is cut to an exact replica of the racing car. Because of an error in cutting the wood, however, this particular wind tunnel car had longer endplates on either side, which extended so far down they nearly hit the ground. This caused the downward pressure to be so great that the sides of the car imploded violently during the testing.

Even as the engineers despaired – renting the wind tunnel was expensive, as was the plywood model, and the lost day of testing wreaked havoc with their plans – Chapman seemed deep in thought. What if that downward pressure – which would later be known as 'ground effect' – that had destroyed this car could be harnessed and turned into something that would actually make Lotus race faster?

Thus was born the 'miniskirt': a longer side plate designed to increase the downward pressure on the car. Chapman's ingenuity helped resolve the most obvious problem, the fact that the longer plates risked hitting the track when cornering, thereby damaging the car and, possibly causing spinouts. He designed the bottom portion of the plates to be made of what looked like brushes, jutting down below the car. They would direct the flow of air, maintaining the 'ground effect' but, because they were flexible, if they did hit the track, the impact on the car would be minimal.

The other teams scoffed at this. In addition to making the Lotus distinctly uglier, they failed to see what benefit the 'miniskirt' could possibly bring. But when Lotus started to take pole positions and win races in the new season, they began to ask questions. And that's when Chapman, realising that the 'miniskirt' was an innovation that his rivals could easily copy with a few months' design work, decided to engage in some old-fashioned misdirection. He encouraged rumours that the secret to Lotus's success was a radical new approach to weight distribution. One of the rumoured side effects was that the car itself could only be raised via an old-fashioned jack applied to the back of the vehicle. To encourage this, Chapman instructed his mechanics to only raise the car in this way: an antiquated and time-consuming method that had no material effect on their work, but which led rival engineers down a series of blind alleys as they tinkered with weight distribution in an effort to replicate Lotus's success.

Lotus won the 1978 Constructors' Championship (and, with Mario Andretti, the Drivers' Championship, too). Realising his rivals were going to catch up, Chapman designed an even more ambitious car for the following season, one which removed the vehicle's 'wings' entirely. Two years later, he introduced a revolutionary dual chassis car. It was his attempt at staying a step ahead, a necessary tactic given that his main rivals were better funded and could do things beyond his reach. In other words, they could do things better. Chapman knew that, if he was going to stay one step ahead, he'd have to do things differently – no matter how much he was derided for daring to be different.

'FROM THE BOTTOM OF MY HEART: I DON'T GIVE A DAMN!'

25

BOBBY FISCHER

We'll let others debate whether chess is, in fact, a sport. Without question though, for Bobby Fischer, it's a form of warfare. And that includes everything that goes into war: strategy, intelligence, recklessness, savagery and folly.

He himself was a child of war and the insanity of Nazism. His mother, Regina, had married a German bio-physicist while studying in Moscow, and gave birth to his sister Joan in 1938. The rise in anti-Semitism under Josef Stalin prompted Regina and Joan to flee first to Paris and then, a year later, with World War II looming, to Chicago. This is where Bobby was born, back in 1943. There has long been doubt over who his father was. Regina was separated from her husband and, according to files unsealed by the FBI (who had investigated her in the 1950s for her communist sympathies), he had never entered the United States. The FBI posited that Bobby's biological father was a Hungarian mathematician based in Chicago, Paul Nemenyi.

Either way, soon after his birth, Regina, Joan and Bobby moved to New York. In 1949, when he was six years old, his mother bought a chess set (complete with instructions) in a sweet shop. Bobby quickly taught himself to play and, in the space of a few months, ran out of viable opponents. Aged just seven, he was one of dozens of children allowed to face the Scottish master Max Pavey in a 'simultaneous exhibition': one of those events where a top chess player faces multiple opponents at the same time, walking from board to board. Bobby lost that day, but despite being one of the youngest participants, he hung in there for more than fifteen minutes, drawing a crowd of onlookers.

Defeat galvanised him: he had finally found a challenge. His fame grew in chess circles and he was known not just for his ability, but for his daring, take-no-prisoners style. A match against International Master Donald Byrne when Bobby was thirteen became one of the most talked-about games in history. Bobby sacrificed his queen early, drew his expert opponent into a trap, then unleashed a battering that left Byrne with no escape.

Just over a year later, aged fourteen, Bobby won the US title without losing a single game. He ached to face ever-better opposition. That meant going to face the top chess masters in the world, most of whom, however, were behind the Iron Curtain. Visas were nearly impossible to come by at the height of the Cold War. Regina wrote to the Soviet leader, Nikita Kruschev. To her surprise, Kruschev consented, if only for the publicity. The Fischers could not afford the airfare, so Regina got creative. Bobby's fame in the US got him invited on to a television game show. Regina accepted – in exchange for return tickets to Moscow.

Once in Russia, Bobby faced a variety of top Soviet players, albeit all in unofficial or 'speed' games. He wanted to face Mikhail Botvinnik, the reigning World Champion. When his request was denied, Bobby flew into a rage and his mood darkened. He began railing against his Soviet hosts, calling them 'Russian pigs'. The Soviets, understandably, took great offence, not least because he was their guest. Fearing for his safety, Regina took Bobby to Yugoslavia.

That experience helped fuel a deep hatred in Bobby for the Soviet Union. In 1962, he accused the Soviet players of colluding to stop him from becoming World

Champion. Fischer maintained that they agreed draws among themselves in order to preserve their ranking and conserve energy for when they faced him. He became so incensed that he virtually retired from chess, not playing a single game for nearly two years. When he returned to competition, he made headlines with his bizarre, paranoid behaviour: he insisted on playing with a lawyer at his side and randomly selecting time clocks, so they could not be rigged against him.

But in 1972, Fischer was ready for another attempt at becoming World Champion. The fact that his opponent, Boris Spassky, was Russian, meant that Fischer himself became something of a pawn in the Cold War between the United States and the Soviet Union. He had never beaten Spassky before. The 'neutral' venue was Reykjavik, Iceland, and it was to be a best-of-five clash over three months, from July to September.

Fischer lost the first two games and was ready to throw in the towel. He booked his return flights home and, as the story goes, was packing his bags when he received a phone call from none other than Henry Kissinger.

'You're going to stay. You're going to play. And you're going to win.' Kissinger's message was simple and direct.

For some reason, Fischer, who usually hated authority, acquiesced. He won the third match. And the fourth. And the deciding fifth as well, completing a legendary comeback that stunned the chess world. The 'Match of the Century', as it was dubbed, had become a giant propaganda tool: first for the Soviets, then, when the tide turned, for the Americans. Fischer could have gone home and revelled in the glory, perhaps taken the opportunity to build his wealth. After all, for the first time ever, his games had enjoyed wall-to-wall coverage and he was a household name. Instead, he virtually disappeared. For nearly two decades he wasn't heard from: he even refused to defend his title three years later.

In 1992, he came back on to the scene, agreeing to play a tournament in Yugoslavia that would see him take on Spassky once again in a rematch of their clash in Reykjavik. But Yugoslavia was under a United Nations embargo at the time and the US State Department informed him that if he went, he risked forfeiting his US citizenship.

Fischer's response? Not only did he go, but at the first press conference, he spat on his US passport and the letter from the State Department. Nobody was going to tell him what to do. He duly beat Spassky and disappeared once again, occasionally returning to the public eye with public pronouncements that ranged from the anti-Semitic to the downright offensive (like when he applauded the 9/11 attacks). By that stage, his genius had slipped into folly. Perhaps for a man who, for most of his life, cared little about what others thought and – apart from Kissinger's phone call – only listened to one voice (his own), madness was always a step away.

'YOUR SCARS ARE WITNESSES THAT YOU NEVER GAVE UP. YOU ARE A HERO.'

26

ABEBE BIKILA

Abebe Bikila was born in the village of Jato, in what is now Ethiopia but was then an autonomous kingdom in the Ethiopian empire. Thousands of miles away, on the very same day, the legendary Argentine Juan Carlos Zabala won the marathon at the 1932 Los Angeles Olympics.

Abebe moved to the capital, Addis Ababa, and joined the Imperial Guard, who, among their other duties, served as bodyguards to Emperor Haile Selassie. He had always loved running, and he continued to do so, often running twelve miles a day. His habit caught the eye of a man named Onni Niskanen, a Swede of Finnish descent who had moved to Ethiopia at the request of the Emperor to help train the Imperial Guard.

Niskanen encouraged Abebe to compete in the Ethiopian Armed Forces championships and he acquitted himself so well that Niskanen began training him with the aim of competing in the Olympics. Initially, Niskanen wasn't sure of the best event to train for, but his mind was quickly made up when Abebe raced in his first marathon in July 1960 in Addis Ababa, coming in first place. Shortly thereafter, he ran another marathon and achieved a time that was faster than the existing Olympic record, held by the legendary Emil Zátopek.

Niskanen had no doubt: Abebe was ready and could spring a surprise at the Rome Olympics in September. It wasn't just his record-breaking time; it was the serenity and calm with which he approached the race. This was evidenced again in Rome in Abebe's reaction to what, for another runner, would have been a catastrophe. Together, they bought a pair of running shoes shortly after arriving in the Italian capital. The problem was, the shoes didn't fit right, and Abebe soon developed blisters. He simply shrugged and announced: 'I'll be running barefoot instead.'

Problem solved.

Abebe was told to look out for Morocco's Rhadi Ben Abdesselam, the favourite. Niskanen asked Abebe to shadow him and, for much of the race he did just that. With just over half the race gone, Ben Abdesselam pulled away from the pack, with Abebe matching his every stride. The others melted away and the two men were side-by-side right until the very end, when, with 500 metres to go, Abebe sprinted away from his exhausted rival. He had set a new world record and, after crossing the finish line, he proceeded to run in place. He would later say that he could have run another ten kilometres or so and that, in fact, it was the instructions he'd been given that had slowed him down. Had he just run his race without worrying about Ben Abdesselam, who knows how much faster he would have been.

His was the first Olympic gold for sub-Saharan Africa, and Abebe returned home a national hero. The emperor gave him a Volkswagen Beetle as a reward and made sure to include a chauffeur, as Abebe did not yet have a driving licence.

He won Olympic gold again four years later, in Tokyo. He wasn't the favourite coming in, partly because nobody had ever successfully defended their Olympic gold medal in the marathon, and partly because he'd had his appendix removed in an emergency procedure just a month earlier. On the flipside, this time he had shoes that fitted properly and, more importantly, he didn't have to worry about shadowing a dangerous rival. He just ran his race, which meant taking off just before the halfway mark and leaving the rest of the field behind.

He won by more than four minutes, then, as in Rome, ran in place and performed calisthenics at the finish line while he waited for the other runners. He may well have won a third Olympic gold in Mexico City in 1968, but a hairline fracture in his fibula forced him to drop out during the race. Nevertheless, he would retire with an incredible record, having won twelve of the sixteen marathons he entered.

Were the story to end here, his achievements would be inspirational enough. He was the dominant long-distance runner of his time and he blazed a trail for a generation of sub-Saharan African runners. But it doesn't end here. In 1969, having finally obtained his driving licence, he crashed his Beetle in Addis Ababa. The accident initially left him paralysed from the neck down. He received eight months of treatment, eventually regaining the use of his arms.

Grateful to the doctors who had treated him and determined to be an example to others, Abebe took up Paralympic events, competing in everything from archery to table tennis and even sled-dog racing in Norway. He died prematurely, aged 41, but his legacy – from the iconic barefoot run through the Eternal City, to his universal charisma as Africa's first global superstar athlete, to the work he did after his accident – will endure forever. Like the plateaus of rural Ethiopia, where it all began.

'THERE ARE
TWO TYPES OF PAIN,
ONE THAT HURTS YOU
AND ONE THAT
CHANGES YOU.'

27

BEBE VIO

She wanted to kill herself. Beatrice Vio – known as 'Bebe' – was ready to end it. She had just returned home from hospital and reality had hit her. Both her legs had been amputated at the knee, and both her arms just below the elbow. As she lay in her bed, she realised that nothing would ever be the same. She was eleven years old and she didn't see life as worth living in that condition.

But in her situation, suicide was practically impossible, especially at that age. She crawled to the edge of her bed. Maybe she could throw herself to the ground. Her father, Ruggero, stopped her. He grabbed her by the shoulders, looked her in the eye and said: 'Bebe, throwing yourself off the bed won't kill you. All it will do is hurt you. And then you'll cry some more and complain to me. If you really want to do it, just tell me. We're on the second floor, I'll open the window and you can jump from there. I'm pretty sure that would get the job done . . . but now stop it. Life is good. Life rocks. Life is really cool.'

Bebe tells that story with a giggle these days, her smile lighting up her face through the scars. In 2008, she was suddenly hit by a virulent strain of meningitis. She was a little girl of eleven. She complained of nausea and head-aches, but by the time the meningitis was diagnosed, it was too late. Doctors at the hospital in Padova, in the northeast of Italy, felt they had no choice but to amputate her limbs to save her life.

Once she accepted her dad's affirmation that 'life is cool', the little girl, who had loved fencing, became determined not to give it up. She was told it was virtually impossible for amputees like her to fence: that they simply couldn't 'feel' the foil, its nuances and moods. But Bebe felt them. Fencing ran deep within her: it wasn't just in her hand and forearm. And so, with a special prosthetic, she began to fence and compete, at first in a wheelchair, then later using her prosthetic legs.

Bebe was too young to compete at the 2012 Paralympics in London, but she was nevertheless chosen as Italy's torchbearer. Around her she saw Paralympic athletes faced with challenges of every kind: each inspired, each inspiring, each pushing the boundaries of technology, hard work and the power of determination.

That only inspired her further. She became the European champion two years later, the world champion in 2015, and won gold at the 2016 Rio de Janeiro Paralympics. And, because inspiration is a spinning wheel, she chose to share hers with others. She is a tireless advocate for both Paralympic sport and early vaccination.

What goes around, comes around. And Ruggero was right. Life is really cool. Really, really cool. Especially when you give back as much as Bebe has.

'SMOOTH SEAS
NEVER MADE
A SKILLED SAILOR.'

28

JOHAN VAN DER VELDE

It was one of the most dramatic stages of the Giro d'Italia and some argue it should never have been run. The year was 1988 and the organisers decided to reintroduce a 75-mile mountain stage that hadn't been part of the itinerary in nearly three decades: from Chiesa in Valmalenco to Bormio, rising up through the 2,621 metres of the Gavia Pass. It's a stage that is as picturesque as it is brutal. The reason that it hadn't been part of the Giro for many years is that the weather, even in early June, can be entirely unpredictable.

And that can make the stage downright dangerous, particularly the four-kilometre descent after the Gavia, which runs over an unpaved stretch of road. On the morning of the stage, black clouds gathered atop the pass and organisers agonised over whether or not to race.

'It's showbiz: let's do it,' was the verdict.

As soon as the stage took a turn up the mountain, a lanky Dutch cyclist named Johan van der Velde took off like a locomotive. He was thirty-two years old. A decade earlier, he had been one of the most promising newcomers to the sport, but his career had never worked out as planned: he never became a star. Instead, he made a living in cycling as a mountain-stage specialist, and as a pacer for more illustrious riders. Years later, we would discover why. His inability to live up to the expectations of others had driven him to amphetamine and gambling addictions. He also had a tendency to engage in petty theft. Van der Velde was later caught breaking into a showroom to steal lawnmowers, as well as attempting to force open a postage stamp vending machine, all in the name of supporting his habit.

But none of this was known at the time. All the other riders knew was that stages like this one were the perfect chance for van der Velde to shine. Early on in the ascent, he discarded his jacket and raingear. It was cold – and would get even cooler at the top – but the adrenaline was such that he felt his extra gear only slowed him down. And it would have. All we know is that he powered up the mountain like a man possessed, even as it started snowing: first flurries, then larger flakes, then, by the time he neared the top, a full-blown blizzard.

By that point, confusion reigned. Van der Velde was far ahead of the peloton, who proceeded with caution, partly due to the snow, partly due to temperatures that reached minus four degrees Celsius. The teams' race cars struggled to keep up as they made their way up the mountain. So too did the motorcycle-mounted cameras, which were broadcasting the race. The pictures they managed to beam back into people's homes were erratic and unreliable.

At the top of the climb, van der Velde was greeted by a crowd of spectators who had overnighted at the Gavia. Some implored him to stop, saying that the descent would be too dangerous, the road reduced to a two-metre wide stretch of white snowdrift and brown mud. Others tried to give him a jumper or a jacket as he flew past them, his legs pumping, wearing only his cycling shorts and a short-sleeved racing top. Confusion reigned as the organisers considered stopping the race. Van der Velde ignored them all, and his decision to go hurtling down the mountain made their minds up for them. It was too late to stop the race now.

This is where the story gets fuzzy, because by this stage, the TV cameras had lost him. What we do know is that, at some point on the descent, van der Velde realised that his muscles were seizing up, his fingers were no longer responding to his commands and his whole bike was shaking. Hypothermia was setting in. (One rider, Dominique Gaigne was even worse off: he had to be carried into a shelter while still on his bike, because his hands had frozen to the handlebars.)

As he sped down the mountain, hitting speeds of 50 miles per hour, van der Velde realised that he had no control over his bike. Frostbite was imminent. He somehow brought the bike to a halt with his feet and, as the story goes, sought refuge in a campervan by the side of the road.

Meanwhile, American Andy Hampsten, a minute or so behind him, was also struggling, but far better equipped. Hampsten's team, fearing the weather might be bad, had visited a ski shop to purchase base layers, coats and other cold-weather gear. They were waiting for him en route. Hampsten must have passed van der Velde at some point, albeit without seeing any trace of him. Hampsten would go on to finish in second place, behind Erik Breukink, who caught him in the final kilometres. Hampsten still made history that day, however: partly because of his team's ingenuity and partly because, after this stage, he became the first American to wear the Giro's coveted pink jersey as overall leader.

And van der Velde? Again, we simply don't know for sure. One story is that he found a French family inside the campervan. They gave him a stiff drink and a couple of heavy jumpers and sent him on his way. He eventually made it to the finish line a full forty-eight minutes after the winner but was nonetheless feted as the hero of the stage.

If there's fine line between bravery and folly, he had crossed it several times on that snowy June day.

'START WHERE YOU ARE. USE WHAT YOU HAVE. DO WHAT YOU CAN.'

29

THE 'WITCHES OF THE ORIENT'

What do you do when you're undersized and overmatched? When you play a different version of a sport? When your country is still on its knees less than two decades after a brutal war which concluded with atomic bombs being dropped on two of your cities?

You get intense. And you get creative.

Hirofumi Daimatsu understood this better than most. He was obsessed with volleyball, having played it at amateur level, and was now a women's coach. There wasn't much demand for coaches in women's volleyball and, indeed, Japan was still rebuilding after World War II. But Daimatsu persuaded the Nichibo corporation, a textile company, that they should put together a company team, and that he should lead it. He told them it would be good for morale, while bringing them prestige and free advertising.

That was in 1954, less than ten years after the Hiroshima and Nagasaki bombings. Daimatsu got to work on a shoestring budget but with plenty of enthusiasm and single-mindedness. Within a few years, Nichibo came to dominate the women's game in Japan, and he became the coach of the national team as well.

Suddenly, everything became more challenging. For a start, Japan played a version of the sport called 'nine-man' which, as the name suggests, involves nine players per side. The rest of the world played six-a-side. What's more, his players were considerably smaller, on average, than their opponents at international level. Blocking at the net, a staple of volleyball defending, was very difficult for them. So too was spiking, especially from further back.

So Daimatsu got creative. He focused on his players' strengths rather than worrying about their weaknesses. They were smaller, yes, but also extremely agile. They would become the best around at defending – not at the net, but at floor level. Diving to save spikes is something that requires courage and quickness. They had plenty of both, and Daimatsu exploited it.

But he did it with a twist. At the time, after a player took a dive for the ball, he or she was usually briefly out of the action, because getting back up took time. Daimatsu invented the so-called 'rolling dive' in which, even as a you stretch for the ball, you make sure you fall with a roll so that your momentum allows you to get right back up. To do this correctly, you have to know how to fall – in this, perhaps he was inspired by his country's martial artists, for whom falling correctly was paramount in order to be able to lessen the impact and continue fighting as quickly as possible.

The 'rolling dive' had another key benefit. When you roll, the ground absorbs much of the blow, which lessens the risk of injury. This was crucial, because it enabled his team to practise diving, something most of their opponents rarely did, as they did not want players getting injured. While other teams viewed diving as little more than an emergency measure, Daimatsu made it the centrepiece of his team.

He also realised that, because of their lack of height, his team had to find non-traditional ways to score points. And so, he emphasised the serve. Today, a volleyball serve in the hands of a talented player can be a devastating weapon; back then, it was mostly simply about getting the ball safely over the net. Daimatsu developed spinning serves and floating serves – again, staples of the game today, but largely unknown at the time. These confused opponents, making a return very difficult.

The flip side was that mastering this required practice. Endless, gruelling practice. He made sure Japan's best volleyball players got jobs with Nichibo so that they could be together year-round, then he put them through a brutal regime. During the week, they worked from 9 a.m. to 4 p.m., then trained from 4.30 p.m. to midnight, with only short breaks for meals. At weekends, they trained from 10 a.m. until 5.30 p.m. They got no more than one or two weekend days off per month.

Daimatsu was very clear with his team. 'This will be difficult and painful and exhausting and unpleasant. If you're not up to it, please leave now. But if you are up to it, you will be giving your team and your country the best possible shot at a gold medal. Is this cruel? Yes. But it is necessary. Superior willpower and work ethic can overcome physical shortcomings.'

His simple message yielded almost immediate results. Japan participated in the volleyball world championships for the first time ever in 1960 and finished as runners-up. The rest of the world was stunned and dubbed them the 'Witches of the Orient'. Meanwhile, Daimatsu came to be known as the 'Demon Coach' for the way he glared at and harangued his players.

Two years later, they dominated the World Championships. Not only did they win all ten games, they lost only one set. They went into the 1964 Olympics in Tokyo as uber-favourites. Olympic volleyball was making its debut and the entire country – keen to bounce back and show the world it had put the past behind it – willed them to a dramatic gold medal.

Daimatsu's methods were always staunchly defended by his players – except for one, who would later complain (to the Japanese prime minister, no less) that the long hours spent training had prevented her from meeting a husband. But Daimatsu had warned them – and he had proven a point. The combination of willpower and creativity can take you to near limitless heights.

'IT'S HARD TO TRUST
THE MESSAGE
IF YOU DON'T TRUST
THE MESSENGER.'

30

JOHN LANGENUS

The year was 1930, and the giant figure doing calisthenics on his own on the deck of the cruise ship taking the Belgian national team to the inaugural World Cup in Uruguay wasn't a player, but a referee. At six feet, three inches John Langenus was an imposing figure, especially by the standards of the day, and one of the best-known referees in Europe.

Which, to be fair, wasn't saying much, since there were no European club competitions, no European Championships and so not much call for international referees, other than the odd friendly between nations, which was usually an ad hoc affair. Still, he had officiated at the 1928 Olympics, taking charge of the bronze medal game and, in an age of amateurism, could afford to take several months off to travel halfway around the world.

Indeed, while Jules Rimet had big plans for his World Cup, the reality is that many nations outside South America showed little interest. There was too much uncertainty, it was too expensive, and nobody knew if a football World Cup was even viable. Rimet had to personally cajole and plead with European nations, and eventually persuaded Belgium, France, Romania and Yugoslavia to participate. And, since he needed neutral match officials, Langenus came along as part of the Belgian 'package'.

Langenus, ever the gentleman, officiated his games

dressed in a wool cap and plus fours, as was the custom at the time. He exuded calm, and his stature ensured respect, but that wasn't enough to spare him some rough-and-tumble moments. In the semi-final between Argentina and the United States, a member of the US team's medical staff rushed on to the pitch to confront him. When Langenus ignored him and told him to leave, the US doctor threw his box of medicine to the ground, smashing many of the bottles inside. One of them contained chloroform and, within minutes, the fumes caused the doctor to collapse. Langenus simply shook his head as the medic was helped off the pitch.

The final pitted hosts Uruguay against arch-rivals Argentina. Rimet had to choose the referee personally, and he had a bit of a problem. Such was the ferocity of the competition between the two finalists, he realised he needed a European refereeing crew to avoid any possible accusations of bias. He approached Langenus, but was rebuffed. The ruckus with the Americans in the semi-final had been unpleasant enough. Langenus had been threatened by the Argentines and was likely to get more of the same from the Uruguayans as well. To him, these were foreign, violent, scary people from a faraway land. This wasn't just about sport: this was a rivalry so vicious, and people so violent, that it was closer to war. At least, that's how Langenus saw it. He just wanted to go home; he'd had enough of this strange land with its demented passion for football.

Rimet insisted. There was no other option. He'd agree to all of Langenus's conditions if it meant avoiding the embarrassment of not being able to stage the inaugural World Cup Final. And so Langenus came up with a list of demands.

He asked that FIFA not announce that he'd be officiating until kick-off. That way, he thought, anybody wishing to threaten the referee wouldn't know which of the dozen or so officials would actually take charge of the game.

He wanted a notary so that he could write a last will and testament, just in case something happened to him. He obtained assurances that FIFA would provide a pension to his wife and children if he suffered a debilitating injury or, worse, was killed in the course of officiating the final. He wanted an armed police escort to the match and a car waiting for him, also with armed policemen, to whisk him away immediately afterwards. Where? Why, to the harbour, where a passenger ship was due to set sail just an hour after the match. His bags would be waiting on board in his cabin.

Rimet agreed, but there was one final stumbling block. When the FIFA tailor presented him with his uniform for the final – black suit, plus fours, black hat and black tie – Langenus protested. 'This looks like the outfit of a man who is about to be lowered into his grave!' he said. A compromise was reached. A referee not wearing black was unthinkable but, at the very least, Langenus would wear a striped tie, rather than the black one.

On the day of the final, Montevideo was abuzz, and the Centenario stadium was packed hours before kick-off. Langenus arrived shortly before kick-off – so soon before, in fact, that Rimet was nervous that he would not make it. Langenus's armed escort had left him in the stadium forecourt – he was concerned that he would stand out and would be recognised as the referee if fans saw him arriving with police in tow – and he made his way to the officials' gate, where he was greeted by stadium security.

'I am John Langenus, the referee for this match,' he proclaimed. 'Please let me in.'

'Oh yeah, nice one . . . that's one we've heard before. You're the thirteenth person today who's tried to pull that stunt,' they told him, before leading him away to a detention area, packed with dozens of people. Some were rowdy fans, some had tried to force their way in and, indeed, several had come dressed as referees.

Langenus began to panic. Because he had insisted on secrecy, very few people knew he had been selected: just a couple of FIFA officials, who were probably already up in the directors' box with Rimet, and his assistants for the day, but no doubt they were somewhere in the referees' dressing room, waiting for him to show up. He started to panic and began to seriously worry that he might not be able to leave the country, let alone officiate the final.

Then, as luck would have it, through the open door of the detention room he spotted a familiar face: the FIFA tailor, the same man who had dressed him the day before. He would know who Langenus was and how, on this day, he had one of the most important roles in football. Langenus shouted to him through the throng and, fortunately, managed to catch his eye: being six foot three in a room filled with smaller people no doubt helped!

The tailor rushed to him, understood the situation and made sure he was released. The game somehow kicked off on time, although not without controversy. Each of the teams, suspecting foul play, had brought their own ball and insisted that it be used. Langenus's solution was to use the Argentine ball in the first half and the Uruguayan one in the second. It's probably a coincidence, but Argentina were two-one up at half-time and eventually lost, four-two.

At the final whistle, the home crowd exploded with joy, but Langenus scarpered out of there as quickly as he could. The arranged transport was waiting for him – except it wasn't a car, but a motorcycle with a sidecar. He folded his large frame into it and off they went to the harbour and his waiting ship. Once on board, he locked himself in his cabin and waited.

By that stage, World Cups and football were the last thing on his mind. Luckily, that mind changed, and he went on to officiate in two more World Cups.

'DO I NOT DESTROY MY ENEMIES WHEN I MAKE THEM MY FRIENDS?'

Abraham Lincoln

31

JESSE OWENS

Jesse Owens hadn't signed up to become a tool in someone else's propaganda war. He was simply an athlete who dominated track and field and wanted to win a gold medal or two (or, as it happened, four). But as the 1936 Berlin Olympics approached, it became evident that the stakes were high.

Adolf Hitler, the German Führer, had turned the Games into a showcase for his demented theories on race and his belief in the superiority of what he called the Aryan people. Owens, an African American and already a world record-breaking athlete, stood in his way – and the world cheered him on.

In fact, his popularity and fame were such that even Germany seemed to embrace him, much to Hitler's consternation. Upon his arrival in Berlin, Owens was greeted by crowds cheering his name. Shortly thereafter he was visited by Adi Dassler, who would go on to found Adidas. He insisted that Owens wear his shoes. Owens would later become the first black athlete to sign a shoe deal with Dassler's company.

Owens duly won gold in the 100-metre and 200-metre sprints. Sandwiched in between them was the long jump: the event that, perhaps more than any other, would give hope to the world. As with many tales from that era, fact and fiction blend together in retellings of this story, but that doesn't make the message any less powerful.

The long jump pitted Owens against the local Wagnerian hero, Luz Long. Most observers felt it would be a tough event for Owens. The tall, blue-eyed Long had the crowd behind him; he was experienced and he was one of the best in the world. Early in the competition, Owens fouled on two consecutive attempts. Was it nerves? Was it the track? Was he trying to do too much? Whatever the case, he was one poor jump away from being eliminated from the competition.

Owens has given different versions of what happened next. In the most often-cited narrative, Long approached him and suggested that he take his jump from a bit further behind the take-off board, in order to avoid the risk of a foul. He could still easily make the qualifying distance; there was no need to take a chance. Owens gratefully took the advice, qualified for the later rounds without incident and went on to win the gold ahead of Long.

Owens himself told the story to Long's son, Kai, in a 1964 documentary by Olympic filmmaker Bud Greenspan. It's a powerful story about selflessness, brotherhood and the Corinthian spirit. But it may not be true.

There is no reliable footage of that stage of the competition, but there are contemporaneous accounts from journalists present who claim that Long never approached Owens. And Olympic historian Tom Ecker, who asked Owens directly about the story in 1965, was told that he only met Long after the competition.

In many ways, though, it doesn't matter. It only makes what happened next much more powerful. Immediately after Owens beat Long to the gold medal, Long embraced him, the first to congratulate him on his victory. The two athletes – white and black, German and American, Aryan and African – posed together and waved to the crowd. It was the ultimate slap in the face, not just to the Führer, but to Nazi ideology.

'It took a lot of courage for him to befriend me in front of Hitler,' Owens would later say. 'You can melt down all the medals and cups I have, and they wouldn't be a plating on the twenty-four carat friendship I felt for Luz. Hitler must have gone crazy watching us embrace.'

Owens won a fourth gold medal in those Olympic Games. He and Ralph Metcalfe were late replacements for Sam Stoller and Marty Glickman in the 4 x 100-metre relay. It seemed like a strange decision by the United States team, as the existing 4 x 100 quartet had great chemistry. Glickman would later allege that the US Olympic Committee, headed by Avery Brundage, made the decision because he and Stoller were Jewish and it would have been a further humiliation for Hitler and the host nation if Germany was beaten by Jews as well as African Americans. Owens initially refused to take part but was ultimately left with no choice.

And Long? The friendship endured. Even though they never saw each other again after Berlin, Owens and Long wrote lengthy letters to each other. This continued even as Long was drafted into the Germany army and sent to fight on the Eastern front. In what would be his final letter to Owens, just before he was killed in 1943, Long wrote: 'Someday, find my son and tell him about how things can be between men on Earth.'

Owens fulfilled Long's request, meeting his son years later. They had spent just a few hours in each other's company, but their bond of respect and friendship would endure and serve as a beacon of brotherhood.

'IN A WORLD WHERE YOU CAN BE ANYTHING, BE KIND.'

32

EUGENIO MONTI

Eugenio Monti wasn't even supposed to be a bobsledder. Skiing was his sport and he was exceptionally good at it, twice becoming Italian champion by the age of twenty-two. He was dubbed 'the Flying Redhead': a tribute to his flaming hair, but also the aggression and intensity with which he faced the slopes.

But two ligament injuries robbed him of skiing before his twenty-fourth birthday, so he turned from the ski to the sled. He quickly discovered that, if you understand snow and slopes and you love speed, your skills will translate from one sport to the other.

He won silver medals in the two-man and the four-man bobsleigh at the 1956 Winter Olympics, held in his native Cortina d'Ampezzo. The following season he became world champion in the two-man bobsleigh, a title he would win seven times, in addition to two world titles in the four-man competition.

When the 1964 Innsbruck Winter Olympics rolled around, Monti was determined to win the gold medal that had eluded him in Cortina in 1956 and been denied him in 1960 (when the bobsleigh event was excluded from the Games). He was, naturally, among the favourites in the two-man bobsleigh competition and was well-positioned after the first few runs. That's when he came across his

British rivals, Tony Nash and Robert Dixon. The pair were agitated to the point of desperation.

He asked what was wrong and they told him they'd probably have to retire from the race. They had lost the bolt that kept together their sled's posterior axis. They had numerous spare bolts, but none that would fit.

It may seem strange to hear today, but back then Olympic teams were hardly the military-style line-ups they are these days, when armies of assistants and mechanics ensure the logistics are perfect. Nash and Dixon were responsible for looking after their own equipment and they were realising they did not have the replacement bolt they needed.

Monti and his partner on the two-man bobsleigh, Sergio Siorpaes, realised their sled used exactly the same bolts as the British team's sled. What's more, they had plenty of spares. Monti took a couple and gave them to Nash and Dixon. They shook hands, and he said: 'May the best team win.'

As it turned out, it wasn't Monti and Siorpaes: it was Nash and Dixon. Monti's team finished third, behind another Italian team. What's more, after the race, Monti was given a hard time by the media. Why had he helped the rival team? And if he wanted to be altruistic, shouldn't he at least have considered the feelings of the other Italian duo, who also lost out to Nash and Dixon?

'Nash didn't win because I gave him our bolt,' he said afterwards. 'He and Dixon won because they were faster than everybody else.'

His teammate Siorpaes went so far as to say: 'I don't even think he thought twice about it. It didn't occur to him that he was doing something special or kind, he was simply doing what came naturally.'

Monti's actions did not go unnoticed by the International Olympic Committee. Alerted by none other than

Nash and Dixon, they chose him for their inaugural Pierre de Coubertin medal. Named for the founder of the modern Olympics, it is a special recognition awarded to athletes who exemplify the spirit of sportsmanship at the Games.

And perhaps there was some karmic value to his sportsmanship, too. Four years later, at the 1968 Grenoble Winter Olympics, when he was forty years old and, according to many, well past it, Monti finally won his gold medal in the two-man bobsleigh. A few days later, he won another in the four-man competition.

He would retire with six Olympic medals in total. But it's a safe bet that the one that, in some ways, meant the most was the Pierre de Coubertin medal.

'NO ONE CAN WHISTLE A SYMPHONY. IT TAKES A WHOLE ORCHESTRA TO PLAY IT.'

33

VALERIY LOBANOVSKYI

The struggle between the individual – with his or her potential for extemporaneous genius – and the collective – with the whole becoming greater than the sum of its parts – has long been a theme in team sports. And it's one that Valeriy Lobanovskyi was all too familiar with, because he had lived at both ends of the spectrum.

Growing up in Kiev in the 1950s, he stood out both athletically and academically. He received a diploma in thermal engineering and trained as a plumber in the post-Stalin Soviet Union. But it was his skills on the pitch, in particular his ability to dribble and deliver seemingly impossible trajectories and curls when striking the ball, that made him stand out. It wasn't purely an innate skill: to make a football twist and turn in flight like a billiard ball, you need to strike it in just the right spot, with just the right part of your boot, and with just the right force. There was something very scientific and precise in the way Lobanovskyi did it, and he revelled in practising and studying new trajectories.

There was another, equally important, influence on the young Lobanovskyi: his manager at Dynamo Kyiv, Viktor Maslov. Maslov possessed an innovative tactical mind and was one of the first to introduce the concept of 'pressing'. Up until that point, when teams didn't have the ball, they would normally retreat and focus on defending. With

Maslov's idea of 'pressing', losing possession was the cue for his players to aggressively advance and try to win it back from the opposition. It was active rather than passive, and it caught many by surprise.

Lobanovskyi, a wide forward, embraced the concept at first. But over time it became apparent to Maslov that, in order to 'press' most effectively, the team had to move collectively. The best way to do this was in a 4–4–2 formation, in which there was no space for a traditional wing like Lobanovskyi. What's more, Maslov's system was predicated on players moving in unison, continually adjusting to each other's positions to ensure that no area of the pitch was left unpatrolled. This meant that attacking players like Lobanovskyi might need to spend long stretches playing deeper and covering for defenders who may have advanced. Lobanovskyi did not object to the sacrifice required of a star player like himself, but it struck him that the emphasis on the system could be counterproductive too. If a brilliant striker like him had to spend long stretches so far away from the opposing goal, did it really benefit the team?

And so, at just twenty-five years of age, he parted ways with Maslov and Dynamo Kyiv, although the experience stayed with him. When, in 1969, he retired and began coaching, he used many of Maslov's teachings. His first club, Dnipro Dnipropetrovsk, was sponsored by the Soviet space programme. He exploited this to spend time with scientists, effectively developing one of football's first sports science programmes. A few years later he moved back to Dynamo Kyiv, this time as manager, and the 'Lobanovskyi method' really took off.

Think of a team as a machine. Which parts are under the most stress? To establish this, he collected data and ran it through rudimentary computers in order to identify patterns of play and the way a team's attacks flowed. If a team is a machine, it also works best when the individual cogs are in the best possible condition. And the cogs, of course, were the players. Together with Anatoly Zelentsov of the Kyiv State Institute of Physical Education, he developed state-of-the-art individual training regimes for each of his athletes, carefully calibrating their workloads to achieve maximum performance when it mattered most.

The impact was instantaneous. Dynamo won the Soviet Double and later the Cup Winners' Cup. This was followed by a resounding victory over the star-studded Bayern Munich, then European champions and a team full of players who had won the World Cup for Germany in 1974. Meanwhile, his centre-forward, Oleg Blokhin, won the Ballon d'Or. Lobanovskyi's success led him to alternate between managing Dynamo and managing the Soviet Union national team, with whom he finished third at Euro '76.

In 1984, he returned to Dynamo. By this stage, his view had evolved. The collective still came first, of course, and the team had to be a machine. But within that, there was room for individual improvisation, for creativity and genius to emerge . . . as long as it created problems for the opposition. In other words, he created a team that Lobanovskyi himself, he of the supreme individual skill set, could have thrived in as a player. One of his team members who benefited was a short, curly-haired playmaker named Aleksandr Zavarov, who married a sense of collective with individual genius to the point that Italian giants Juventus would choose him to replace the legendary Michel Platini a few years later.

Two years later, after winning the Soviet Double, Dynamo again reached the Cup Winners' Cup final, where they demolished Madrid. The respected Spanish newspaper *El Pais* said Dynamo 'looked like a team that had time-travelled from the future'.

For the next four years, Lobanovskyi combined the jobs of coaching Dynamo and the Soviet Union national team to great effect. In the 1986 World Cup, the national team reached the knockout stage only to be defeated in controversial circumstances by Belgium, who overturned a two-nil deficit to win four–three in extra time. And in 1988, they steamrollered their way through the European Championships, only to be felled by a Marco van Basten wonder-strike in the final, losing to Holland.

The fall of the Soviet Union and the chaos that followed forced Lobanovskyi to emigrate to Asia, where he managed the national teams for Kuwait and the United Arab Emirates, helping both win continental silverware. After disappearing somewhat off the European radar, there was to be a third and final act as he returned to a now-independent Ukraine to coach – who else? – his beloved Dynamo Kyiv. He won five league titles in six seasons and once again perfected a system where the collective came first, but individual expression flourished. Once again, Lobanovskyi had combined organisation and genius, two things which, like water and oil, weren't supposed to mix. He passed away after suffering a stroke pitch-side in 2002, immersed in what he loved most: football.

'DREAMS AND DEDICATION ARE A POWERFUL COMBINATION.'

34

SARA SIMEONI

At twelve, Sara Simeoni was a long, thin slip of a girl. She danced and dreamed of being a prima ballerina, but her ballet school in Verona had some bad news for her. Yes, she was graceful and coordinated and had promise. But she was simply too tall: she would later grow to 178 centimetres. Ballerinas can't dance at that size. Not alone, not in an ensemble. There was no future for her in dance.

She slipped into the sort of depression you only get at that age, when you realise that you have been lied to by the world. Follow your dreams and you can achieve anything, they had told her. Nope, not this one. God made you too tall.

So, her parents took her to the athletics track. Maybe there was some kind of sport she could do? Something she'd enjoy? She tried a bit of everything: track events, shot put, long jump, high jump. And it was in the latter that she realised that, without really trying, she was good. Actually, more than that. She was exceptionally good.

It was just a diversion at that stage. Not a dream, like dance had been. But she was good enough to go to the 1972 Olympics in Munich, finishing sixth. And that's where the bug caught her. If she worked as hard at this as she had at dance, if she wanted it badly enough, maybe, just maybe . . . who knows what could happen?

The problem was combining practice with everyday life.

There was one proper high-jump facility in Verona and that was in the football stadium, the Bentegodi. Practising there meant waiting your turn. So, she'd show up, often after dinner, and practise by moonlight.

Her personal best continued to improve. She won a silver medal in Montreal at the 1976 Olympics, reaching 1.91 metres. Two years later, at an Athletics meet in Brescia involving Italian and Polish athletes, the equivalent of a 'friendly' in football, she reached 1.98 metres. It was a new Italian record, but that didn't excite her. Even as she landed on the mat, she realised she had cleared the bar by a substantial amount. She was in the zone: this was her night.

So, she signalled to the judge to put the bar higher, to 2.01 metres. Nobody had ever jumped that high. A deep breath, the usual run up, the leap, the flop and down she came. The bar stayed frozen, unmoved. Not even a tremor.

It was a new world record. Or was it? The meet wasn't televised, and when news spread, the governing body refused to accept it. Yes, there were witnesses, yes, there were judges; but there was no TV. And it wasn't an official event. Plenty disputed her jump. After all, her personal best in competition had been 1.94 metres. How could she possibly have added another seven centimetres?

It was a 'phantom record' – until a few weeks later, that is. Because at the 1978 European Championships in Prague, she took to the field once more and, again, jumped 2.01 metres. This time, the whole world saw it live on television, and there were official judges and adjudicators of every stripe present.

Simeoni had been vindicated. The uncertainty over her record only lasted a few weeks. All those nights by herself, jumping in the moonlight in an empty football stadium had been worth it.

She went on to win Olympic gold in 1980 in Moscow and a silver medal in Los Angeles in 1984. But maybe the best thing came years later, in 2008, when she received a call from a small, local television station in Brescia. Somewhere in the archives, an old VHS tape had been found. On it was a grainy recording of her jump thirty-two years earlier in that exhibition with the Polish athletes.

By this stage, of course, it was a moot point. But it wiped out any doubt regarding what she had achieved – and when she had achieved it.

'IF YOU ARE MORE FORTUNATE THAN OTHERS, BUILD A BIGGER TABLE, NOT A TALLER FENCE.'

35

ROBERTO CLEMENTE

Puerto Rico has an unusual relationship with the United States. It is a territory of the mainland and, as such, Puerto Ricans are full US citizens. And yet it has no representation in US congress and Puerto Rican residents do not have a vote in the presidential elections. Add in matters of race and language and you can see why the island felt so far away from the mainland when Roberto Clemente burst into Major League Baseball.

He had been a baseball phenomenon from a young age in Puerto Rico and arrived in the United States just a few years after Jackie Robinson broke the colour line. In fact, Clemente's own team, the Pittsburgh Pirates, had only started featuring black players the season before and there were still a number of teams that remained staunchly all-white. In Clemente's case, there was another barrier that left him further isolated: he did not speak English.

Indeed, in his early years not only did he endure racism due to the colour of his skin: his language skills were often ridiculed, with reporters quoting him phonetically in the newspapers: 'Me like hot weather, veree hot.' But Clemente's sense of duty, humility and professionalism only drove him on, and he soon gained everyone's respect. He was voted on to the All-Star team for twelve seasons and won four batting titles. Along the way, he became only the eleventh player in baseball history to record 3,000 hits.

Yet as important as his baseball career was, Clemente kept himself busy in the off-season. He knew how important his success was to Puerto Ricans and he freely gave up his time (and often his money) to help the islanders, both those back home and the many who had emigrated to the continental United States.

Two days before Christmas in 1972, a terrible earthquake hit Managua, the capital of Nicaragua. Clemente had been there earlier that month and received a rapturous reception. Baseball was the number-one sport in Nicaragua and, as a fellow Latino excelling in the United States, he had been adopted as a national hero.

He immediately got to work arranging aid packages of food and water to be sent, and chartered three different flights to the Nicaraguan capital. It was typical Clemente. Soon, though, word got back to him that much of the aid he had organised and paid for had gone missing, stolen by corrupt officials and sold on the black market.

Deeply disturbed by this news, and with no hesitation, he decided that he himself would join the next aid flight to Nicaragua. Nobody would dare steal in his presence. He was too famous, too respected. He chartered a DC-7 cargo plane, packed it full of supplies and took off on New Year's Eve from Puerto Rico, bound for Managua.

A young baseball player he had been mentoring, Tom Walker, helped him load the plane. Walker offered to fly with him, but Clemente declined. 'You're young, go and party for New Year's instead,' he said.

The plane crashed shortly after take-off and there were no survivors. But Clemente's example of humility, philanthropy and duty continues to inspire. Since his death, Major League Baseball, has named an award, which recognises players for outstanding community, work after him.

No fuss, no publicity. Just humility and a tremendous sense of duty . . . and one of the game's greatest-ever players, to boot. That was Clemente.

'SEEK RESPECT,
NOT ATTENTION.
IT LASTS LONGER.'

36

ANNA KOURNIKOVA

If you play poker, specifically Texas Hold 'em, you may know what an 'Anna Kournikova' is. An ace plus a king is a hugely attractive hand – if you play it right. Many inexperienced players don't, however, because they tend to overplay it. They're blinded by the strength of the ace–king opening and become more aggressive than they should be. And they lose.

It's unclear where the term originated, but beyond the obvious – Kournikova's initials, AK – there's a certain parallel there. When Anna Kournikova burst on to the scene in women's tennis, she looked like a sure thing. Born in Moscow, she joined the Spartak Tennis Club (whose alumni include Elena Dementieva, Yevgeny Kafelnikov and Marat Safin), where she was coached by the legendary Larisa Preobrazhenskaya. At age ten, Anna moved to Bradenton, Florida, to live and train at another much-heralded academy: that of Nick Bollettieri.

She made her debut at the US Open at the age of just fifteen and reached the fourth round, losing to the reigning number one in the world, Steffi Graf. The media hype surrounding Kournikova immediately went into overdrive. She was tall, athletic and elegant in her strokes, but she was also extremely attractive. In fact, for several years, her name was one of the most searched on the internet.

The following summer she made her debut at Wimbledon,

reaching the semi-final, where she lost to Martina Hingis. And then her career began to stall. Her propensity for unforced errors – which many believed she would iron out of her game as she gained experience – reared its head, as did various injuries, primarily to her back. She would eventually break into the women's top ten in 2000, albeit briefly, never rising higher than eighth.

Some called her soft. Some questioned her character. Some wondered whether she was simply a media creation, owing to her stunning looks. And, truth be told, she could easily have lived off her looks, perhaps with a career in modelling or personal appearances. She had a string of famous boyfriends, from hockey stars Sergei Federov and Pavel Bure, to pop singer Enrique Iglesias. She would have had no trouble trading off her celebrity status for the rest of her life.

And maybe that's where the 'Anna Kournikova' poker hand fits the narrative: attractive, full of potential, but generally a loser. Except that's not what happened.

With great humility, Kournikova rededicated herself to her tennis. Not so much in the singles game, but rather in doubles. It's easy not to fully appreciate what this took. When all you knew was your meteoric rise and the success others had thrust upon you, measuring yourself up and acknowledging your limitations takes quite a bit of introspection.

But she loved to compete and she loved tennis, despite what her critics thought. And she proved it. She teamed up with Hingis, her old rival, and won two Australian Open titles. In fact, she achieved the number one spot in doubles. For someone who was always forced into the limelight, sharing it with someone else halved the burden and the pressure. But, equally, it takes a selflessness to be a team player, especially when everybody had you pegged as a lone superstar, outshining everyone else.

'NO ONE CAN MAKE YOU FEEL INFERIOR WITHOUT YOUR CONSENT.'

37

MICHAEL PHELPS

Michael Phelps's mother, Debbie, was told by a frustrated teacher that her five-year-old son would 'never be able to focus on anything'. The little boy was a ball of energy, always fidgeting, always moving, always needing to be the centre of attention. He was difficult to teach and disruptive towards other students which, in turn, made it difficult to teach them. An educational nightmare, in other words.

A few years later, Michael would be diagnosed with ADHD (attention deficit hyperactivity disorder) and, like many other kids in the mid-1990s, he was prescribed Ritalin, a powerful pharmaceutical.

He was tall and gangly, all limbs, with ears that stuck out to the point that some called him 'Spock'. He was exhausting in every way, which is why Debbie was so grateful that, when he wasn't wreaking havoc in school or on the playground, he was in the pool.

Michael, like his older sisters, was a competitive swimmer from an early age. The evenings after swimming practice, when he returned home mentally and physically exhausted after three hours of all-out effort in the pool, too tired to act up, were often the only respite Debbie got.

One day, she realised that things didn't quite add up. Michael's mind was, supposedly, all over the place: he couldn't concentrate and couldn't focus, right? So then why was it that he could swim endless laps, sometimes for two or three hours at a time without interruption, practising the same stroke over and over and over again?

Together with the family physician, Debbie realised that being in the pool calmed things down for her son more than the Ritalin. Phelps himself would explain this, years later, in his autobiography.

'Once I figured out how to swim, I felt so free,' he wrote. 'I could go fast in the pool, it turned out, in part because being in the pool slowed down my mind. In the water, I felt, for the first time, in control.'

And that, ultimately, was what his ADHD was about: control. Together with other therapies, the swimming helped Phelps regain control. He had the capacity to concentrate and focus on his technique for long stretches, but only in the right context. Over time, he was able to take that focus with him outside the pool as well.

It may never have worked out that way if not for his coach, the legendary Bob Bowman. A tough taskmaster, on the surface he didn't seem an ideal fit for a hyperactive kid like Phelps. But within the confines of the pool, he was the yin to Phelps's yang: pushing him, smoothing out the edges and helping him grow outside the water as well as in it.

When they met, Bowman told Phelps that, if he was willing to listen, he could make the 2004 Olympics. In a way, Bowman wasn't quite right: Phelps actually made the 2000 Olympics, and every Olympics after that for the next sixteen years. Along the way, he won twenty-three gold medals, including eight in a single edition of the Games, at Beijing in 2008. This broke the record held by Mark Spitz, which dated back to 1972. Phelps is the most decorated Olympian of all time.

These days, Phelps runs a foundation that helps children with ADHD conquer their hyperactivity through swimming. As for the 'focus' thing, Phelps addressed that when he said: 'The more you dream, the further you get.'

'PRACTISE LIKE YOU'VE NEVER WON, PERFORM LIKE YOU'VE NEVER LOST.'

38

EDDY MERCKX

'The race is won by the rider who can suffer the most. Anybody who thinks it came easy for me is wrong. Nobody knows just how much pain and suffering I endured.'

Judging by his 525 career victories over eighteen years, it's a safe bet that, if what Eddy Merckx says is true, nobody on two wheels can match his suffering. The young daughter of a teammate nicknamed him 'the Cannibal' because he refused to let anybody else win if he could at all help it. Merckx never liked that moniker, but he was downright insatiable when it came to being the first across the line, and would go to any lengths to be number one.

His training sessions were legendary, and he would often clock up more than 300 kilometres on a daily basis. And to think that, these days, he probably wouldn't have even been allowed to race: when he was twenty-two, he was diagnosed with non-obstructive hypertrophic cardiomyopathy, which basically meant he was at much-heightened risk of a heart attack every time he got on a bike.

But for him, that's all there was.

'Training,' he said, when asked his secret. 'Training, training and more training. The more you ride, the more your mind strengthens and helps you deal with what you'll face in a race. It's that simple.'

Legend has it that he'd go through some fifty bikes a year, mostly because of the tremendous stress his day-long rides would put them under. They simply weren't designed to be ridden that hard, that long. Because, of course, only the Cannibal would do that to a bike.

He never let up. His critics might have said it was ego, he said it was simply competitiveness and professionalism.

'I know I'm good,' he said. 'And if I'm at a race, the organisers, the fans, the other riders, the sponsors, they expect me to compete at my hardest. If I don't do that, I'm letting them down and I'm letting myself down. And I'm not being a serious professional. Obviously over a three-week race I'm not going to win every single stage. But you can be darn sure I'm going to try.'

In 1969, at the Giro d'Italia, another rider approached him.

'Eddy, are you sure you want to win this again?' he said, before motioning to a briefcase. 'I've been asked to make you an offer, a proposal, if you will . . . Inside this briefcase is cash: a lot of cash. You won the Giro last year. Maybe this year you can take it easy . . . and that money will all be for you.'

Merckx looked at him. 'Put it away,' he said. 'I don't want to know how much is in there or who gave it to you. Whoever it is, tell them I'm not going to do that. I don't race for money. I race to win.'

Two days later, Merckx tested positive for a banned amphetamine and was disqualified. He cried all night. To this day, he protests his innocence, claiming he was set up and his sample mishandled.

'I would have won the Giro that year,' he insists.

Instead, he had to make do with winning it the following year, 1970. And in 1972. And in 1973 and 1974. And these were in addition to the Giro he won in 1968 – plus his five wins in the Tour de France. But the Cannibal, who suffered for his craft, was never sated.

'YOUR LIFE IS YOUR MESSAGE TO THE WORLD. MAKE SURE IT IS INSPIRING.'

39

GEORGE BEST

We yearn for heroes and entertainers. Some make us laugh, some dazzle us, some become symbols for paths we don't take – maybe because we choose not to, maybe because we can't. George Best was all those things and more.

Very little was common or mundane about him, starting with that last name. Born in Belfast, he made his debut for Manchester United at seventeen and became a regular the following year, helping them to their first league title since the Munich air disaster almost six years earlier. United fans were smitten with the bandy-legged winger, who combined an elegance, a refined touch with an often-impudent streak.

He began to make his name in European football, earning the nickname 'the fifth Beatle' on a trip to Lisbon to take on Benfica, a game in which he scored two goals. United won another league title with Best in a starring role and in 1967–8 became the first English club to win the European Cup. Best was one-third of what came to be known as 'the Holy Trinity' – Bobby Charlton, a survivor of the Munich air crash, and Denis Law were the other two – and was seen as the epitome of rebellious cool. That year, Best also won the Ballon d'Or and drew comparisons with Pelé.

Off the pitch, he exuded a certain kind of British cool, both in the way he dressed and the way he carried himself. He owned fashion boutiques and night clubs, and he endorsed a whole range of products. Men wanted to be him, women wanted to be with him, and advertisers wanted him pictured with their products.

But then things began to decline. Sir Matt Busby, who had given Best his debut and assembled the side, left his managerial post. The club made a string of poor signings. Charlton and Law began to age. Best himself was quoted as saying he felt as if he was 'carrying the club'. And on some days, like the memorable FA Cup match against Northampton in which he scored six goals, he truly was.

Best was still in his mid-twenties when partying and a lack of discipline began to really affect his playing. He started missing games and training sessions to spend time with various women. In addition, he was drinking and staying out all night. Best announced his retirement at age twenty-six, changed his mind, got fined and suspended, then disappeared for nearly a month, occasionally getting spotted in various London nightclubs.

He played his final game for United on New Year's Day 1974, kicking off an itinerant decade which would see him sign short-term contracts all over the world, from South Africa to Ireland, from Scotland to Australia, from the English second division to the now-defunct North American Soccer League. He wound up playing parts of six seasons for US teams in Los Angeles, Fort Lauderdale and San Jose.

In some ways, the NASL accelerated his fall. It was a glamour league that attracted big names like Pelé, Johan Cruyff, Franz Beckenbauer and Giorgio Chinaglia, but it was also a paragon of overspending. Often, over-the-hill players were there for just two reasons: partying and pay cheques.

The 1980s were, perhaps, Best's darkest decade. He admitted to picking up a woman just so he could steal money from her to continue drinking, dipping into her handbag when she went to the toilet. He spent Christmas

1984 behind bars, after he was arrested for driving drunk and assaulting a police officer. He was married twice and had a son, Calum, but the two were estranged for much of his life.

Strangely, throughout the 1990s and the turn of the millennium, as his health deteriorated further and he ran into financial difficulties owing to his failed business ventures, the idealised image of George Best, the cheeky, uber-talented rebel who charmed men and women remained strong. One of his most famous quotes brings a smile to most people's faces: 'I spent a lot of money on booze, birds and fast cars . . . the rest I just squandered.'

With hindsight, that quote is probably as tragic as it is humorous. This was a man out of control, a shell of his former self, who much of the world still saw as their own personal entertainer rather than a real person who was slowly wasting away. It's not that people weren't willing to help him. Many tried – and failed. It's more that, by that point, Best was a prisoner to his illness, alcoholism, and to the character he had created.

But there is a redeeming ending to the legend of George Best. As he lay dying in his hospital bed, he invited in the photographers of a Sunday newspaper. They faithfully chronicled his plight, showing him in his final hours, with all the physical ugliness of his condition as his light began to fade. His one request was that they include his final message to the world: 'Don't die like me.'

His final act in life was not to hide his shame, but to expose it to the world so that others may take heed. That day in autumn 2005, just as he had forty years earlier, Best was living up to his last name. Having given the world so much entertainment and joy as a young man, he was able to give them wisdom as a dying man.

'THE MEANING OF LIFE
IS TO FIND YOUR GIFT.
THE PURPOSE IS TO
GIVE IT AWAY.'

40

DICK FOSBURY

Dick Fosbury was sixteen years old when he realised that he had a problem. He was a high jumper, and a determined one – but not a very good one. He was tall and thin and athletic enough that his coaches insisted he had the tools to do it and do it well, but he simply couldn't get the pieces to fit together.

At the time, in the early 1960s, high jumpers basically used one of two techniques. One was the 'scissors': you ran at the bar at an angle, jumped, and lifted your legs over the bar, first one and then the other.

The other method, which was becoming increasingly popular at the time, was the 'straddle' or 'roll' method. This was more difficult, as it involved throwing yourself at the bar and going over it face-down, with your body parallel to the ground. It required timing and coordination as well as speed and physical strength.

Fosbury practised both and found he wasn't suited to either technique. He simply couldn't get the required body control to master the 'straddle', and the 'scissors' could only get him so high before one or the other of his long legs caused the bar to tremble and fall.

Still, he persevered with the 'scissors' and, slowly, began tweaking the technique. He realised that, by taking a more extreme angle, he achieved greater height, effectively twisting his body in the air and going over the bar head-first.

This also allowed him to get an extra kick while airborne, which helped steer his trunk over the bar.

Except there were two problems. The first was that his coaches didn't like it – and neither did the coaches of his opponents. It looked ugly and uncoordinated, with Richard Hoffer comparing it to 'an airborne seizure'. When his method proved to be effective, others questioned whether it was legal. It was; the only requirement in the high jump is that the jump be taken off a single foot, not two.

The other issue was, potentially, far more serious. If you go over the bar on your back and come down head-first, you'll land on your head. In an era when most landing areas for the high jump were made of wood chip, sand or sawdust, that meant running the risk of breaking your neck with each and every jump.

This is where luck and circumstances changed history. Fosbury's high school happened to install a foam rubber mat as a landing surface at around this time. This enabled him to continue to train and perfect his new technique. It still carried risk and, in fact, when he competed elsewhere, it was often on sand or sawdust. Indeed, he injured his back on several occasions, compressing vertebrae.

Once Fosbury was at university, though, his coach would have none of it. This was not how serious high jumpers approached their sport. If he was going to compete at Oregon State University, he was going to do it right. That meant learning the straddle technique that had so bedevilled him in high school. Fosbury spent hours working on the straddle, but found more time to continue practising his own technique too. And when, in his second year, he set a new school record using his own method, his coach became an instant convert.

He encouraged Fosbury to work to perfect his style even further. He changed the angle of his run-up, he kicked out his hips at the top of his arc, effectively adding to his time

163

in the air, he took off from further away. All these little tweaks were the result of trial and error, as well as painstakingly studying video recordings of his jumps.

The results were staggering. Fosbury went to the 1968 Mexico Olympics and returned with the gold medal, as well as a new Olympic record. Within a few years, most of the high-jumping world had switched to the 'Fosbury Flop'. It would never have happened without Fosbury's passion, creativity and determination to become a competitive high jumper. But there was another reason, one that was very simple and entirely out of Fosbury's control: the introduction of foam rubber landing surfaces. Without them, there would be no Fosbury Flop.

'WHY BE NORMAL
WHEN YOU CAN BE
AMAZING?'

41

CHRIS EVERT

'Ninety per cent of my game is mental. It's my concentration that has got me this far.'

That's how Chris Evert explained her success. And while she was perhaps being a bit modest when she famously said she was never much of an athlete, there is no question that concentration and single-mindedness are at the heart of everything she does.

'To be a tennis champion, you have to be inflexible,' she once said. 'You have to be stubborn. You have to be arrogant. You have to be selfish and self-absorbed. Kind of tunnel vision, almost.'

She was like this from a young age, ever since her father, Jimmy, a former professional, took her and her siblings out on the clay courts in their native Fort Lauderdale, Florida. She was like a robot, she recalls: 'Wind me up and I would play on and on.' She favoured a two-handed backhand, which gave her more power and would ultimately become one of her hallmarks. Most of all, she could outlast most opponents, hitting every shot back with eerie consistency. She never gave up; she always kept going, like a perpetual motion machine.

She turned professional at fourteen and, three years later, reached the semi-final at Wimbledon, where she was beaten by the defending champion, Evonne Goolagong, who came back from being down 4–6 and 0–3. After the match, an exhausted Goolagong said the secret to her comeback was realising that Evert's groundstrokes, while consistent, were often neither hard nor deep, leaving her vulnerable to drop shots.

Even without Goolagong pointing it out, Evert probably knew what the chink in her armour was. So, she doubled down. She worked tirelessly to make her shots deeper, more angled, tougher. And she worked on her fitness, her ability to cover the court, even against drop shots or physically bigger and stronger opponents.

Two years later, in 1974, Evert won her first Grand Slam tournament at Roland-Garros, the French Open. It would be the first of eighteen Grand Slam tournament wins in a seventeen-year career. Along the way, she went undefeated on clay for six years, spanning 125 matches.

She also found herself as one half of one of the greatest rivalries in the history of sport, pitted against Martina Navratilova. It is hard to say whether Evert's grit and single-mindedness would have been so extreme if not for the challenge of besting her Czech-born arch-rival. The pair were a study in contrasts: Navratilova's powerful, athletic, serve-and-volley game against Evert's drip-drip baseline consistency.

At one point, between 1982 and 1985, Navratilova beat Evert in thirteen consecutive matches. And so, Chris did what she had done before. It's not so much that she worked harder – she was already maxed out in that department – but that she worked smarter and differently, just as she had done more than a decade earlier, when she taught herself to vary her ground game and eliminate her vulnerability to drop shots.

Evert changed coaches, changed training methods and, to some degree, changed her style of play, picking her spots but becoming more aggressive in her forays to the net. In 1985, at a Virginia Slims event in Florida, she beat Navratilova in straight sets. Not only that – she beat her on a hard court, her rival's preferred surface. Fluke? Off-day for Navratilova? The sceptics leaned in that direction, by no means convinced. Evert would have to do it again in a major tournament.

A few months later, that is just what she did. Once again, it was the French Open. Predictably, they met in the final. Evert won in an epic three-set thriller, winning the third 7–5. She regained the number-one spot in the world, and the media and public loved it.

Because when it came to the 'Chris vs Martina' rivalry, most sided with Evert, especially in the United States. Some called her 'Chris America'. Navratilova was the naturalised foreigner, the tall powerhouse who lacked Evert's grace. Perhaps Evert's aesthetic appeal helped her popularity too; with her porcelain skin, elegance, blonde hair and princess-like demeanour, she had a conservative, good-girl look that many lapped up. As the *Washington Post*'s Tom Friend put it: 'Chrissie was a beautiful woman playing a beautiful sport in a beautiful way. And that's why America fell in love with her.'

But in some ways, it was an act. None other than John McEnroe said: 'She was an assassin that dressed just nice and said the right things and meanwhile cut you to shreds.'

And perhaps, as she once said, it was mostly in the mind.

'99% OF THE BATTLE IS GETTING YOURSELF IN THE RIGHT FRAME OF MIND.'

42

MUHAMMAD ALI

The script for 'The Rumble in the Jungle' was written way before that night in late autumn, when George Foreman and Muhammad Ali entered the ring in Kinshasa. By that stage, the storyline was set and the actors had to play their part. Two of them – Ali and the promoter, Don King – were already legendary salesmen. The third, Foreman, was one too, although we wouldn't discover it until years later when he began flogging his grill across all media.

Multiple tales were spun. There was the classic underdog yarn: Ali, by this point, was most definitely not the favourite, having lost against both Joe Frazier and Ken Norton. Foreman was the undefeated World Champion, who had won thirty-seven of his forty fights by knockout.

Ali was the maverick, the rebel who had been to prison for his beliefs, the man who spoke truth to power. And then there was Foreman, the choice of the Establishment. He had grown up poor but had benefited from government programmes such as the Job Corps to become a carpenter and, in his spare time, a boxer. He was an Olympic gold medallist who the media held up as a hero who stayed out of politics, focusing on sport and entertainment. The fight soon came to be seen as the clash between the man with the courage to speak out and the man who kept his head down, bowed to the system and reaped the rewards.

Their styles also helped define them. Ali was the entertainer, the elegant boxer who floated like a butterfly and stung like a bee. Foreman was seen as a puncher, a strong, one-dimensional brawler. And he revelled in it, once saying: 'Boxing is like jazz. The better it is, the more most people dislike it.'

Then there was the broader storyline. King's idea – deemed folly at first – to stage the fight in Zaire fuelled the narrative of African American fighters going back to their roots. In a racially polarised United States, it spoke to the fact that black Americans could rely on themselves and their kin back in Africa. In fact, much of the decision to hold the fight there was to do with King's struggle to find venues that could meet his demands in the US. But the idea of leveraging his relationship with the Zairean dictator Mobutu Sese Seko and getting the Libyan leader Muammar Gaddafi to bankroll the fight was pure genius. It was the developing world giving the world's superpower the middle finger.

So entrenched was this message that when Foreman arrived to train in Zaire, some were surprised to discover that he was black and of African descent. They were expecting a privileged white boxer, because that fitted the tale that had been spun.

Even if he had been Kinshasa-born and -bred, it would have been tough for Foreman to compete with Ali's massive popularity. And, to be fair, Foreman didn't help himself when he showed up with his beloved German Shepherd, exactly the same kind of dog that Belgians had used to terrorise the Congolese during their brutal colonial rule.

Ali, of course, milked it all as best he could. He led the crowd in chants of 'Ali, *Bomaye!*' ('Ali, kill him!'). He ran through the streets, followed by huge crowds. He never once failed to remind the media why they were in Africa and what this meant.

For all the bluster from Ali, once the fight began – at 4.30 a.m. local time, to suit television audiences back in the

United States – the crowd saw a different man. Foreman advanced and Ali seemed to turn himself into a human punchbag, absorbing blow after blow. And while it looked like the script was being followed – the uber-favourite was on top – it was, in fact, all part of Ali's plan. He did get hit a lot, but they were either glancing blows or, more commonly, punches that struck him when he was in a protected stance, often leaning against the ropes. Why does that matter? Because being hit when up against the elastic ropes meant he wasn't absorbing the full power of the punch. Rather, as the writer Norman Mailer put it: 'the rope . . . receive[d] the strain'. Thus, the rope-a-dope technique was born.

Foreman huffed and puffed his way through the match, raining blows down on Ali, but doing little effective damage. In fact, the champion was merely tiring himself out and, as the fight went on, leaving himself open to Ali's lightning-quick counterpunches – and the vicious left hook that nailed Foreman in the eighth round, sending him to the canvas.

Ali had triumphed. He had fooled the crowd, fooled the worldwide audience and, most importantly, fooled his opponent. He had created and written his own story and had triumphed by playing to his own rules.

'GREATNESS IS EARNED NEVER AWARDED.'

43

JIM THORPE

They could not have been more different. The King of Sweden, presiding over the 1912 Olympic Games, born to regal privilege and noblesse oblige. And the Native American orphan, who had lost both parents and a twin brother before he turned 18, raised between ranches and labour camps for mixed-race children masquerading as 'boarding schools'.

That day in 1912, when King Gustav described Jim Thorpe as the 'greatest athlete in the world,' it is said that the man known as 'Wa Tho Huk' – or 'Bright Path' in the language of the Sac and Fox Nation – simply grinned and said 'Thanks, King!'

Despite his name, Thorpe's path had taken him through plenty of darkness before exploding into the light at the Stockholm Olympiad. And it would later veer into the shadows once again.

Thorpe was born in Indian Territory in what is now Oklahoma, although no record exists of his birth: just a baptismal certificate with a date he himself disputed. One of his grandfathers was Irish, the other French, but both his grandmothers were Native American: Potawatomi and Sac and Fox. He was raised among the latter. His twin brother, Charlie, died aged nine; his mother, Charlotte, a few years later. Life was tough on the reservation. Jim's relationship with his father deteriorated, and from the age of twelve the young Jim ran away regularly, sustaining himself through odd jobs. Just a few months before his father's death, they were reconciled. Jim ended up at a trade school for Native Americans in rural Pennsylvania. It was the sort of place the government set up as a last-ditch attempt to save marginalised young men from an unmoored, drifting and potentially dangerous future.

Sport hadn't been on his radar – it rarely is when survival is your main objective – but one day in 1907, he walked past a high jump competition at the school. He was intrigued and asked if he could have a go. Dressed in street clothes, he promptly set a new school record. Thus began a staggering career that saw him compete in baseball, lacrosse, football and, yes, ballroom dancing, where he was one half of the 1912 intercollegiate championship team. (It was also how he would meet his first wife, Iva Miller.)

He loved football and concentrated on that in college, where he was named All-American (an honorific title given to the best players in the sport) for three straight years. He didn't even compete in athletics for two years but, with the 1912 Olympics on the horizon, he was persuaded to return to the track. What wasn't clear was which sport he would choose to compete in. Simply put, he excelled at nearly everything.

And so, he was entered into the pentathlon and the decathlon, while also qualifying for the long jump and high jump. The pentathlon was almost too easy: he won four of the five events and placed third in the javelin (although he had an excuse: he had never even picked up a javelin until a few months earlier). He also won four of the decathlon events, setting a record that would stand for some twenty years. And, competing against specialists in the long jump and high jump, he finished fourth and seventh.

The world was at his feet. King Gustav was so impressed he awarded him a special trophy to go with his medals.

He returned as a national hero. His path was illuminated from all sides.

And then darkness fell. It emerged that, while at university, Jim had been paid to compete in some preseason baseball games. Rules at the time were steadfast: only amateurs could compete in the Olympics. Professionals were seen as a debasing the Olympic spirit, and Jim was stripped of his medals.

He went on to play professional baseball, football and basketball, while also starring in Hollywood movies. But the stripping of his medals remained a blow to his pride. He struggled later in life, working in construction and security to make ends meet and even enrolled in the Merchant Marine in his late fifties. He died in 1953.

Jim Thorpe's legacy means his path returned to brightness years later. In 1983, the International Olympic Committee reinstated his medals. The US Postal Service put him on a stamp. Two towns in Pennsylvania merged and renamed themselves 'Jim Thorpe' in his honour. And his story served to educate many about the hardships faced by Native Americans, many of whom were not even recognised as US citizens until the 1920s. Even after his death, through ups and downs, his path veered to the light.

'NO MATTER HOW GOOD
YOU GET YOU CAN
ALWAYS GET BETTER
AND THAT'S THE
EXCITING PART.'

44

WILT CHAMBERLAIN

What struck you first about him was his height, obviously. Standing seven feet one inches, Wilt Chamberlain towered above others, even in the National Basketball Centres of his day. But then, if you saw him move, you were struck by something else: how could someone so big also be so coordinated, so fast and, above all, so physically strong?

Chamberlain's first love growing up wasn't basketball, but rather track and field. In high school, he broke the state record in the 800 metres, and in college, excelled in the shot put and high jump. But it was on the hardwood court that he dominated in a way that we will probably never see again.

Statistics only tell part of the story, but in Chamberlain's case they are so extreme, you can't ignore them. He holds no fewer than seventy-two NBA records. He has the mark for most points per game in a season (50.4), as well as the next three highest point-scoring seasons in history. Bear in mind that Michael Jordan and Kobe Bryant, two of the greatest players ever, only managed to score fifty or more thirty-nine and twenty-eight times respectively in their entire careers. He also boasts the single-game record for rebound (fifty-five) and the mark for most rebounds per game in a season (27.2). To date, he is the only player ever to lead the league in both scoring and rebounding in the same season . . . and he did it on six occasions.

Then, of course, there's the small matter of his 100-point game, which he achieved in 1962. Often, even entire NBA teams don't reach 100 points in a game. For one man to score that many is unfathomable. Chamberlain holds six of the ten highest single-game scores ever recorded, and his 100-point game is well ahead of the second highest, Kobe Bryant's eighty-one in 2006.

When you dominate to that degree, one of two things can happen. You either become universally adored or you become a hate figure. Chamberlain ended up as the latter. He was Goliath, but there were very few Davids around who could topple him.

'He is not an easy man to love,' the owner of one of his teams, the San Francisco Warriors, once said. 'Wilt is easy to hate . . . people came to see him lose.'

To be fair, Chamberlain did bring some of it on to himself. He could be a bit of a diva: while playing in Philadelphia, he chose to live in New York, commuting down in a chauffeur-driven limousine each day. He also insisted that daily practice be moved to the afternoon – four o'clock – because he liked to sleep late and, in any case, had to drive the 100 miles or so from New York city each day. His nightlife, in the meantime, was legendary and he was known to drive from games in Philadelphia straight to Manhattan nightclubs. In fact, in his autobiography, he would boast of having slept with more than 20,000 women in his career.

The fact that such an outstanding sportsman would only win two NBA titles (the latter coming at the very end of his career) was also seen as evidence that he was not a team player. His critics said he lacked leadership and was simply an egomaniac determined to pad out his own stats.

But in 1966, something changed: something that would end up silencing many of Chamberlain's critics. A man named Alex Hannum took over as coach of the Philadelphia 76ers and immediately took Chamberlain to task.

Hannum had no fear of the hulking Chamberlain and regularly berated him, saying he should 'act like a man'. On more than one occasion this led to physical confrontations, with the entire team needing to step in to separate the two. But Hannum won Chamberlain's respect. This was one person who was not afraid of him and, truth be told, such people were few and far between in basketball circles.

Chamberlain knew that while everyone respected his ability, not everyone respected him as a winner. And while almost everyone feared him, he also knew that most hated him. And so, he listened to Hannum, who told him that it was time to change his style of play.

Hannum asked him to focus more on defence, on helping teammates guard opponents: until that point, it appeared to many that Chamberlain was content with simply rebounding and not letting his direct opponent score. And, crucially, he told Chamberlain that he could be a devastating passer, and should look to provide assists to teammates, rather than shooting each time he got the ball.

The logic was simple. Chamberlain was so athletic that every time he stepped outside the paint, the opposition had a difficult choice to make. They could either send the tall player who was guarding him under the basket out into the open, in which case the middle would be open for one of Chamberlain's teammates to run into and receive the pass; or they could guard Chamberlain outside with a smaller, faster player, but that meant it was child's play for Chamberlain to pass the ball over that player's head.

Hannum's plan worked. Chamberlain, the consummate scorer, turned into an exceptional passer, finishing third in the league in assists and, the following year, leading the NBA in the category. Most importantly perhaps, the Sixers won the NBA title in 1967 and only narrowly lost in the finals the following year.

People took Chamberlain's immense physical gifts for granted, dismissing them as God-given. This is unfair and absurd, because even with all that talent, you don't achieve what he achieved without drive, intensity and work ethic. But they couldn't fault the transformation he underwent in turning himself into the leading assist-man in the NBA. That was all on him: that took humility and putting the team first. And it showed them how wrong they all were about him.

'HARD WORK PUTS YOU WHERE GOOD LUCK CAN FIND YOU.'

45

STEVEN BRADBURY

At one point, it became part of the lexicon: 'Doing a Bradbury'. In other words, reaching a goal that was as unexpected as it was improbable. Not because you hadn't worked for it, but simply because it seemed so far out of reach.

It owes its name to a man named Steven Bradbury. And while, in the popular narrative, he was a 'Mr Nobody' who came out of nowhere to win a gold medal, that's not quite accurate. He was a short-track speed skater who had won medals in the 5,000-metre relay in three different World Championships in the early 1990s and, in 1994, had won bronze in that same event at the Lillehammer Winter Olympics. That success earned him his place in history because it marked Australia's first ever medal in the Winter Olympics.

He was considered a talent in his early twenties, but a horrific injury at a World Cup event in 1994 appeared to derail everything. During a race, another skater's blade sliced through his right thigh following a collision and Bradbury lost four litres of blood. He ended up with 111 stitches and it took him a full eighteen months to return to action.

Misfortune seemed to follow him everywhere. In 2000, he broke his neck in a training accident after he crashed headfirst into the barriers to avoid a fallen skater. He was in a halo brace for six weeks and had metal plates bolted to his back and chest. He was told he would never skate again, not even recreationally.

But Bradbury was single-minded, and determined to prove them wrong.

He put himself through a punishing workout routine and returned to competition in time for the 2002 Winter Olympics in Salt Lake City. He was a rank outsider but, simply by being there, he had proven his point. He was, once again, a competitive short-track speed skater.

And that's when luck – so often his enemy in the past – came to his aid. He finished third in his quarter-final heat and figured his Olympics were over, as only the top two skaters would go through to the next stage. But Marc Gagnon, the defending World Champion, was disqualified for obstructing another skater, and Bradbury advanced to the semi-final.

It was here that his strategy changed somewhat. Realising he could not compete with the others in terms of raw speed, he took another approach. Short-track speed skating is a rough-and-tumble-affair, with tight turns in small rinks, with room for only four to six skaters. Falls and collisions are inevitable. Rather than go all out, Bradbury opted to hang back a little, conserve his energy and hope those at the front got in each other's way.

And that's what happened. Three skaters who were well ahead of him all crashed, while another was disqualified, allowing him to sneak past them into first place – and into the final, much to everybody's shock. There was no reason to change his strategy at this stage. The other competitors were much faster than him, but, equally, there was a fierce rivalry among them. What's more, they were all under extreme pressure to win, as Bradbury would later acknowledge. He knew the chances of one of them getting carried away and making a mistake were real. The odds of all of them making mistakes, though, were very low.

Predictably, he was way behind throughout the race. As they approached the final turn, there were a good fifteen metres separating Bradbury from the four leaders: Mathieu Turcotte of Canada, Apolo Anton Ohno of the United States, Ahn Hyun-Soo of South Korea and Li Jiajun of China. But then, as they jostled for position, they all fell away. One slipped and slid off to the right, another fell, taking the other two with him. Bradbury, who was placidly skating behind them, overtook them all, literally two or three skates from the finish line.

They had been 'Bradburied'. But while he acknowledged his good fortune, he also made the most compelling of points: 'It didn't take me a minute and a half to win gold: that was just the time it took in the race. It took me ten years to get here.'

'HARD WORK BEATS TALENT WHEN TALENT DOESN'T WORK HARD.'

46

WORLD CUP 1950

In the narrative of football, one match, perhaps more than any other, stands out as a kind of parable of arrogance. England, the country who had invented the sport, had never shown much interest in the World Cup, at least not until after World War II. In fact, the Football Association declined to participate in the first three editions of the tournament. And, when they eventually did take part, at the 1950 World Cup in Brazil, it was half-heartedly. After all, they felt they were so far ahead of the rest of the world that there was surely little to be gained from beating other nations trying to play football.

That's why the Football Association arranged a goodwill tour of Canada, which overlapped with the start of the 1950 World Cup. It really didn't matter that Stanley Matthews, their best player, missed the opening victory against Chile, 2–0. He wasn't needed. And while they made plans to have him join the side for their second match, against the United States, the FA's selection committee insisted he would not be needed and he wasn't picked. After all, why change a winning team? Besides, it was only the United States . . .

And, in fact, you can understand their dismissiveness. The US team was made up of amateurs and semi-professionals. The goalkeeper, Frank Borghi, drove a hearse. The captain, Walter Bahr, was a teacher. There were dishwashers, paint-strippers and even a postman. They had lost their last seven competitive internationals by a combined score of 45–2. The *Daily Express* scoffed that it would be 'only fair' if the USA were given a three-goal lead at the start of the match, like a handicap in golf.

By contrast, the England team, despite the absence of Matthews, could still count on the likes of Billy Wright, Stan Mortensen, Alf Ramsey and the legendary Tom Finney. They played and trained at the highest level: they were the ultimate All-Star team of their day.

Yet there was also a psychological element to the USA team's performance that day. Most of the team had been drawn from the country's various immigrant communities: Portuguese, Italian, Irish and German. These were first- or second-generation players taking the opportunity to represent their new country in the sport of their old country. Several of them, like Eddie McIlvenny and Joe Gaetjens, weren't even US citizens yet, but were on a path to naturalisation. They had the enthusiasm of the converted: and that mattered.

In the same way, there was a psychological element to their opposition's performance. Maybe it wasn't by design, but England were seen as reeking of arrogance. Their sense of entitlement rankled the US players, as well as the largely Brazilian crowd in Belo Horizonte. Bahr, the US captain, handed the armband for this game over to McIlvenny. Proudly Scottish, born and bred, McIlvenny had emigrated to the US two years earlier to join his sister, taking a job in a factory. For a while, he had given up football altogether. Beating the 'auld enemy' probably mattered more to him than anyone. (Later, ironically, he would be called by another great Scot, Sir Matt Busby, to play for Manchester United, the greatest English side of them all – but that's a story for another time.)

No footage exists of the game, but contemporary accounts speak of a one-way battering, with England dominating the match and the US desperately hanging on. Borghi made a string of fabulous saves. There was a sense of inevitability, though: England's goal was surely coming. Except when the goal did come, it came at the other end. Gaetjens deflected a ball past the English keeper, Bert Williams, towards the end of the first half, leaving the English stunned. The rest of the match saw England lay siege to Borghi's goal, but to no avail.

Bahr would later be brutally honest.

'The perfect game is to win and play well,' he said in 2010. 'We won, but we certainly did not outplay England. It was one of those games where the best team does not win. I am proud of it. But if we played England ten times, they would have won nine of them.'

Maybe so. But that's sport. Chance and probability matter. And if you're better prepared, and outwork the opposition, you can spin them in your favour – and pull off the greatest shock in the history of the World Cup.

'GREATNESS IS A LOT OF SMALL THINGS DONE WELL EVERY DAY.'

47

BABE DIDRIKSON ZAHARIAS

Mildred 'Babe' Didrikson Zaharias was so far ahead of her time that she may as well have been a visitor from the future. Growing up in South Texas in the 1920s, the idea of women playing sport felt alien enough, let alone sports that were otherwise reserved for boys.

But she didn't care, and neither did her parents. Both had emigrated from Norway (her three older siblings were born there) and they cared little for local custom. If Babe wanted to play, she could play. And it didn't matter that she was a tomboy who was loud and in-your-face and didn't wear prim and proper dresses. They wouldn't have suited her muscular build anyway. In fact, her one 'feminine skill' – as it may have been considered at the time – proved extremely handy: she was an exceptional seamstress, who would later design her own clothes.

Growing up she regularly competed against – and beat – boys in sports such as basketball and baseball. Those, however, weren't an option at the 1932 Olympics. So, she turned to athletics, where she won a gold medal in both the eighty-metre hurdles and the javelin, while having to settle for silver in the high jump. (Despite equalling her opponent's mark, she was penalised for her technique, which was deemed 'improper'.) She had actually qualified for five events, but Olympic rules at the time restricted women

191

to competing in only three. Who knows how many more medals she might have won?

After the Games, and needing to make a living, she toured the United States with an exhibition basketball team named after her, taking on all-comers. Such was her fame that she was invited to pitch in a Major League baseball exhibition as well.

Many viewed her as a physical freak of nature, others as a sideshow. The sports columnist Joe Williams, writing in the *New York World-Telegram*, was unimpressed. 'It would be much better if she and her ilk stayed at home, got themselves prettied up and waited for the phone to ring,' he wrote.

Still, those who could look past such prejudices saw a phenomenal athlete. None other than Grantland Rice, considered by most the greatest sportswriter of his time, said: 'She is beyond belief until you see her perform . . . then you finally understand that you are looking at the most flawless section of muscle harmony, of complete mental and physical coordination, the world has ever seen.'

Other competitors, while admiring her prowess, were less impressed with her personality. She was uber-competitive and a bad loser, but also self-centred and something of a prima donna. These were qualities that would later become acceptable in male athletes (think Muhammad Ali or Cristiano Ronaldo), but were considered jarring in a woman.

Zaharias was in her mid-twenties when she picked up golf. She was a quick learner, routinely excelling at the sport. Because of her basketball exhibitions, she was considered a professional and denied amateur status, which meant she could not enter any of the women's tournaments (or 'ladies' tournaments' as they were known at the time). So, she entered the Los Angeles Open, a PGA event in 1938, competing against men, many of whom had golfed all their lives. She narrowly missed the cut and, until the mid-1990s, she was the only woman to have competed against men at a PGA event.

Once her amateur status had been re-established, she came to dominate the LPGA, winning ten major titles, including the US Women's Open on three occasions. In 1950, she completed the Grand Slam, capturing the US Women's Open, Titleholders Championship and Women's Western Open.

She was probably the most famous American female athlete of the first half of the twentieth century and, in any case, the Associated Press voted her the greatest female athlete of 1900 to 1950. She was diagnosed with colon cancer in 1953 and, as she did with her sport, faced it head on. She held a press conference to let the world know and became an ardent fundraiser for the American Cancer Society. She continued her golf career, winning the US Open by an incredible twelve strokes. She passed away two years later, but her legacy can't be overstated.

Zaharias became an icon for women in sport and women's liberation in general, despite the fact that she never spoke out on the subject. She let her achievements and actions, and the attitude with which she approached life, do the talking.

'I WILL STOP AT NOTHING UNTIL I ACHIEVE MY GOALS.'

48

FAUSTO COPPI

Alfredo Binda had a problem. A problem of abundance. He was tasked with managing the Italian team at the 1949 Tour de France, back in the day when cycling was divided by nationality, rather than commercial teams. On the surface, his team was stacked with talent, boasting both the defending Tour champion, Gino Bartali (a two-time winner) and Fausto Coppi, who had won his third Giro d'Italia earlier that year (he would go on to win it a record five times).

The issue, however, was that Bartali and Coppi were great rivals. Bitter rivals, even. Binda understood this, having been a top competitive racer himself. He was a three-times World Champion, who, a generation before, had won the Tour twice and the Giro five times (just like Coppi would). Binda knew that, while cycling was a team sport, at the very top, it's a lonely game. You give everything you have to overcome your rival: it's mano-a-mano. Any ounce of energy, mental or physical, that goes to any other competitor is an ounce of energy you're not using to beat your rival.

That's why cycling teams have clear hierarchies. That's why there's a star who is best placed to win and a team of grunts helping him along. Hierarchies can change, of course, and sometimes the star puts his ego aside to help a teammate win. But, generally speaking, there can only be one star.

Except here, clearly, there were two: each with a chance to make history. Bartali had the opportunity to become the first repeat champion in two decades, and only the second man to win three Tours. He was thirty-four at this stage: World War II had robbed him of seven opportunities to win the Tour when he was in his prime. Surely, he deserved the top spot.

Then again, Coppi had the chance of achieving an unprecedented double, winning the Tour and the Giro in the same year. In fact, with the World Championships coming up later in August, he was well-placed to make it a treble.

Binda's solution? 'We'll see.'

Binda's refusal to commit meant that Coppi was reluctant to even participate. He feared that, because Bartali was older and more popular, his rival would end up getting the nod. He only agreed to ride two weeks before the start, and showed up with an obvious chip on his shoulder.

Things went from bad to worse in the fifth stage, when Coppi collided with another rider, the Frenchman Jacques Marinelli, as both veered to grab a bottle of water offered by a spectator. Marinelli got up, realised his bike was fine and cycled off. Coppi's bike was damaged beyond repair. He waited for the nearest team car to roll up with a spare bicycle, only to realise the only one available was set for a rider much shorter than he. After fiddling with the seat for a few minutes, he gave up and sat down by the side of the road. He was crying hysterically.

A team official made things worse when he suggested that the bike did not need to be perfect for him to continue. All he had to do was get to the end of the stage and make up for it the next day. He appealed to his pride: 'You know, this wouldn't be a problem for Bartali. He's so competitive, he would have cycled off even on a ladies' bike.'

It was the wrong thing to say, and it led to a furious Coppi tantrum. Maybe, deep down, he knew it was true.

But at this point, things had gone too far: he was going to quit. Eventually, his spare bike did arrive, but it took a lot of persuading to convince him to finish the stage. It also took Bartali stopping and agreeing to ride alongside him, as a show of support. By the time a grumpy Coppi made his way to the finish, he had lost eighteen minutes that day, leaving him thirty-seven minutes behind the race leader overall. You could never make up such a gap. And he was there to win the Tour, not to bring up the rear.

He went to see Binda and told him he was going home. When Binda objected, Coppi, who knew his cycling history, reminded him that Binda too had once quit a Giro d'Italia because he was so far behind.

'Yes, it's true,' Binda nodded. 'And guess what? I've regretted it every day of my life.' Maybe this planted a seed of doubt in Coppi's mind. But the moment that made his mind up came a few hours later, when he settled in for his post-race massage with a man named Biagio Cavanna. He was a legendary figure on the Tour, a former track cyclist who lost his sight in his early twenties. He retrained as a masseur and physiotherapist, mainly because he wanted to remain in the world of cycling. He was nicknamed 'the blind sage' for his wise advice and was as much psychologist as he was masseur to the riders.

'You're asking what's the point of continuing? I'll tell you,' he said, as he worked Coppi's muscles. 'You still have a chance to show the world who you are. Tomorrow is an easy stage, followed by a rest day. Then, there's a time trial. Stick around. It's ninety-two kilometres: win it, wipe the floor with everyone, then see how you feel. If you still want to go home, that will be fine. If you want, I'll even go home with you to keep you company on the way back.'

It was right to appeal to Coppi's ego and emotions. He didn't just win the time trial, he dominated it. It was the kickstart he needed. At every stage, he clawed back his minutes, closing the gap. Eleven days later, on a long mountain stage, he and Bartali raced away and, by this point, they were first and second. In fact, Bartali was first – largely because Coppi allowed him to win the stage, since it was his thirty-fifth birthday.

But in the next stage, a mountain route from Briançon across the Italian border to Aoste, Coppi had no need to be magnanimous. It was no longer Bartali's birthday. He did stop and wait for Bartali after the former suffered a puncture, but when Bartali fell and hurt his ankle a few kilometres later, Coppi had Binda's blessing to take off. And take off he did, sailing to the finish line with a wide margin that got him the yellow jersey.

He would end up winning the Tour, his first, by more than ten minutes, something that would have seemed unthinkable a few weeks earlier. And, after it was over, he and Cavanna would embrace, both crying. The 'blind sage' had been right. He knew what mattered to Coppi – and he knew the buttons to push.

'SOMEONE IS SITTING
IN THE SHADE TODAY
BECAUSE SOMEONE
PLANTED A TREE
A LONG TIME AGO.'

49

BARON DE COUBERTIN

Pierre de Frédy, Baron de Coubertin, was born into privilege at a time when the old order was changing in his native France. The Second French Empire had fallen and France had been badly beaten in the war with Prussia. He probably knew that, for aristocrats like himself, it was a case of evolve or die.

So, he put his advantages to good use. He studied at the prestigious Sciences Po – one of the *grandes écoles* that churned out members of the country's ruling class – but rather than turning to politics or the military, his interest was drawn to something else: education and pedagogy.

His family's wealth allowed him to travel and he seized the opportunity with great humility, visiting universities and boarding schools throughout England and the United States. What he found surprised him and fed his core belief, which harked back to the old Latin saying *Mens sana in corpore sano* (a healthy mind in a healthy body). These were places where education and physical vigour went hand in hand. Where the mind and the body were one, where physicality wasn't something for the uneducated masses, but for leaders of men and intellectuals, like himself. The young men he observed – remember, back then, in the late 1800s, education was a privilege – were his peers, the future ruling classes.

He came to realise that physical education was a key

element of pedagogy and that France's recent failings on the military front were probably not unrelated to the fact that their leaders, both military and political, were more theoretical than practical. Why? Precisely because, De Coubertin concluded, they had neglected physical education. They were thinkers, not doers.

This notion was only reinforced by his classical studies, particularly when it came to ancient Greece. He was also no doubt influenced by a man named William Penny Brookes, an English physician and botanist who believed physical fitness could stave off a range of illnesses. Brookes organised what he called 'Meetings of the Olympian Class', a series of athletic events in the English countryside. He wasn't the only one. The Liverpool Athletic Club held its own Olympic festivals and, in Greece, the Zappas cousins, wealthy philanthropists, held national versions of the games within their country. There were others as well. These men had been in contact with each other but failed to gain traction. Some had wealth, but not the right connections. Others were very committed to acting locally but could not imagine creating an international – or even national –event. Others, while championing the idea, were too busy with other endeavours.

Somebody was needed to pull all these different elements together. De Coubertin stepped into the fold, cautiously at first, but later becoming the driving force, particularly after a trip to Greece to visit the original Olympic site. He was struck by the sanctity of sport, the simple beauty of the human body pushed to compete and the way it took precedence even over war. The ancient Greeks, the people who had essentially built western civilisations, valued sports and competition. Surely, then, they should be considered alongside the other elements, including art, democracy, philosophy, literature and a range of other pursuits, that form the basis of modern European culture.

De Coubertin set to work and organised a congress at

the Sorbonne in Paris. This congress would eventually become the International Olympic Committee. He knew there would be resistance and mistrust, so he laid on what was, essentially, a marketing spiel. He waxed lyrical about the humanist ideal, about the body and the mind fuelling each other to achieve greater and grander goals. And he propagated the notion that the Greeks, our forefathers, valued the Olympics so much that wars stopped so that young men could compete. This last idea – which has become something of a mantra of the Olympic Movement – was a bit of a stretch. Even in ancient times, wars weren't actually suspended. All that happened was that athletes were given safe passage in order to travel to the games to compete. But, still, the idea caught hold, and fired up the imagination of those present.

That was in 1894. Two years later, the first modern Olympic Games were held in Athens – partly because it was the site of the ancient games, partly because the Zappas family helped fund it – and, at least for a while, Europe's powers set their differences aside and competed in sport, rather than in war and politics.

'WHEN EVERYTHING
SEEMS TO BE
GOING AGAINST YOU
REMEMBER THAT THE
AIRPLANE TAKES OFF
AGAINST THE WIND
NOT WITH IT.'

50

USA ICE HOCKEY TEAM

The Cold War winds were blowing hard over Lake Placid in February of 1980 as the Winter Olympics approached. Herb Brooks, the coach of the US ice hockey team, had an ominous feeling, although he could not have known that things would be getting worse. The United States would go on to boycott the Summer Olympics in Moscow later that year, and the Soviet Union would do the same for the 1984 Games in Los Angeles.

Brooks knew his sport, like a lot of Olympic events, was a weapon: a propaganda tool in the Cold War. At the 1972 Olympics in Munich, the Soviet Union had upset the United States in basketball, marking the first time in the history of the Games that the USA had not won gold in the sport they invented.

In ice hockey, the situation was reversed. The Soviets had won four consecutive gold medals, dating back to the 1964 Games, and were heavily favoured. The United States was home to most of the National Hockey League (NHL), the world's premier ice hockey competition, but the Olympics was reserved for amateurs. In any case, most of the top NHL stars were actually Canadian.

This meant Brooks had to select his side primarily from the ranks of college hockey, picking athletes who had not yet turned professional – or, in some cases, never would, because they simply weren't good enough. It meant relying on younger players, and sometimes less gifted ones.

By contrast, Canada's system of 'junior hockey' churned out a continuous stream of young talent. As for the Soviet Union: officially they were all amateurs, because professional sport didn't exist behind the Iron Curtain. In practice, though, they were professionals: athletes who were employed either by the military or some state-owned company, but actually spent all their time playing and training. It was 'state amateurism' and a huge propaganda boost. It allowed the Soviet government to make it seem as if their sport was purer because their athletes had day jobs and played for the love of sport. This also coincided neatly with the Olympic ideal of amateurism. In fact, their 'day jobs' were shams, no-show gigs that allowed them to earn good salaries, by Soviet standards, while competing at the highest level.

It also meant that their team could grow together over time and develop experience. While each US Olympic team needed to be effectively rebuilt from scratch every four years as players moved on and became professionals, the Soviet side stayed together – and grew together. Five Soviets were returning from the team that had won gold in 1976, whereas just one on the US side, Buzz Schneider, remained from the team that had finished fifth in Montreal. What's more, the Soviets had added stars like Viacheslav Fetisov, Sergei Makarov and Valeri Kharlamov, all of whom would go on to be enshrined in the Hockey Hall of Fame, the sport's highest individual honour.

Brooks knew the Soviet team weren't just more talented; they also had better chemistry, because they played together so often and, in many cases, had grown up together. His team had no such luxury, but the issues of teamwork and chemistry were paramount to him. That's why, as part of the open try-outs he held to assemble his team, Brooks included a 300-question psychological questionnaire. He wanted the best players, sure, but he also wanted guys who could work together, who would put the team first, who could make the whole greater than the sum of the parts. And if that meant, on some occasions, sacrificing individual talent for collective play, so be it.

Both sides played a series of exhibition games against other teams in the lead-up to the Games. In the final one before the tournament, the USSR crushed the USA 10–3 at Madison Square Garden in New York City. Unsurprisingly, expectations were low going into the Games, but the US managed to qualify from the group stage, finishing second behind Sweden. Meanwhile, as predicted, the USSR romped through their group, winning their five games by an average score of 10–2.

The tournament had four teams advancing to the final round with a round-robin format, with the twist that head-to-head results from the group stage would carry over. This meant that the Soviets began the round with two points, Sweden and the USA with one and Finland with zero. The United States would have to beat both Finland and the Soviets to win the gold, something which seemed unfathomable to most.

Before the game, Brooks told his players: 'You are meant to be here. The moment is yours.' They were behind, but not yet eliminated. They could still change history.

The United States went behind twice in the first period but equalised on each occasion. Both times the Soviet goaltender, Vladislav Tretiak, seemed to be at fault, misjudging a long-range effort, then deflecting another seemingly innocuous long shot into the path of an on-rushing US forward. It was here that the Soviet coach made a key decision. He removed the goaltender, Tretiak, widely considered the best in the world, and sent on his back-up, Vladimir Myshkin.

Still, the Soviets dominated the second period, albeit scoring only once, to take a 3–2 lead. And then came the miracle. The Americans equalised again, seemingly out of nowhere, Mark Johnson's shot slipping under Myshkin's body. A few minutes later, following another defensive blunder, Mike Eruzione scored to put the USA in front: 4–3.

There were still ten minutes left to play, an eternity on the ice. The Soviet Union roared forward, but it was here that Brooks decided to be bold. Rather than retreat up the ice and play defensively, hoping to snatch another goal on the counterattack, the USA continued to push forward, as if they were the team chasing the score. It stunned the Soviets, pinning them back for long periods of time. Meanwhile, at the other end of the ice, the Soviets were panicking. They could not believe what was unfolding.

At the buzzer, in a memorable piece of commentary, US sports commentator Al Michaels shouted: 'Do you believe in miracles? YES!'

Momentum from that win propelled the US team past Finland in the final group game, although by that stage the Finns were virtually eliminated and it was almost anti-climactic. Brooks had taught the world a key lesson: even if the wind is against you, use its force to your advantage. And the 'Miracle on Ice' stands as evidence that it can be done.

'THE PESSIMIST
COMPLAINS ABOUT
THE WIND.
THE OPTIMIST EXPECTS
IT TO CHANGE.
THE LEADER ADJUSTS
THE SAILS.'

51

LEBRON JAMES

LeBron James was born to a 16-year-old mother. His father had an extensive criminal record and would hardly feature in his life. LeBron's early childhood involved continuous moves from one public housing project to another. There were many things he could not control in his difficult, deprived childhood. So, from an early age, he focused on what he could control – and he worked it to his advantage.

The most obvious thing was basketball. He was touted as a phenomenon from a very young age: tall, strong, athletic and gifted, but also blessed with vision and unselfishness. He had that Holy Grail quality that coaches crave in any sport: he could make his teammates better.

He was thirteen, in middle school, when he made one of his first conscious decisions over what he could control. He had been playing on a recreational team, the Northeast Ohio Shooting Stars, who had been dominating the region. LeBron and several of his teammates and close friends – Sian Cotton, Dru Joyce III and Willie McGee – were being actively recruited by local high schools, who were hoping that these talented players would enrol and turn their teams into powerhouses. LeBron, of course, was the most highly coveted of all, but he made a pact with the others: 'Nobody can take just one of us, you have to take all four. All for one and one for all.'

This meant that suddenly the quartet, led by LeBron,

had tremendous leverage. Whoever persuaded them to enrol would be getting a new ready-made team. From his perspective, LeBron would be surrounded by close friends and guys with whom he already had great chemistry. He'd have control of the team from day one.

That's how they ended up at St Vincent-St Mary's, a private, predominantly white high school with big ambitions in basketball. They not only won state championships in three of the four years he was there, they also travelled the country to play exhibitions, quickly raising his profile even further. Even during high school, James knew he was ready for the next level. Again, he tried to take control by petitioning to enter the NBA Draft a year before even graduating school, after his third year of secondary education. On that occasion, he was rebuffed – nobody had ever attempted this – but it sent a clear message: he wasn't going to go to college; he didn't need to.

Again, it was about control. The college basketball system is, largely, a transactional one. Universities offer scholarships to the best players, who then play for them for up to four years. This is often hugely lucrative for the universities in terms of television revenue, box office receipts, merchandising and donations from alumni fans. And the business model works because, well, the players don't get paid. The argument for this is that very few players actually make it to the NBA and, by going to college, they at least get an education. From a sporting perspective, high-level college basketball allows kids from high school to develop their game and grow as players.

James knew he didn't need that. He was already there. And, particularly given his background, he didn't feel like playing for free for four years. So, he went straight into the NBA draft and was selected by his hometown team, the Cleveland Cavaliers.

He was an instant success and continued his ascent to superstardom over seven years, taking them to the NBA finals and winning the league's Most Valuable Player award in 2008–09 and 2009–10. But along the way he realised it was time to take control once again. He let his contract wind down and became a free agent, able to sign for any team who made him an offer. Suddenly, it was like 1997 all over again. Just as he and his friends had determined their own future by choosing their high school together, James and two other superstar free agents – Chris Bosh and Dwayne Wade – opted to sign for the Miami Heat.

Cleveland fans were furious. Many saw it as a betrayal, a case of turning your back on your heritage and roots to chase the big contract and glamour of Miami. James seemed oblivious to this and, instead, delivered on his end of the bargain. He won two NBA titles and two more MVP awards in Miami. And, perhaps crucially, he experienced what victory tastes like: something he hadn't enjoyed since high school.

And in 2014, he opted out of his contract with Miami and became a free agent once again. Once again, he was in control. And what did he do? He returned to Cleveland who, without him, had amassed the worst record in the NBA over the previous four seasons. Not all fans were convinced initially, but he came back as an NBA champion and that mattered, both to him personally and to the team on the court.

He immediately took them back to the NBA finals in his first season. The following year, he delivered the NBA title. It wasn't just the Cavaliers' first-ever NBA crown, it was the first title by any professional sports team in the city of Cleveland in fifty-two years. And it was won thanks to a native son. LeBron cried that day, conscious of what he had overcome – but, perhaps, also conscious of the decisions that had brought him to this moment in his life. And the fact that he had been the one to make them.

'IT TAKES A VILLAGE
TO RAISE A CHILD.'

52

FOOTBALL IN ICELAND

It was the fairy-tale story of the 2016 European Championships. Iceland, a nation of volcanos and frostbite a third
of the way across the Atlantic Ocean, between Europe and
North America, had beaten England, 2–1, to advance to the
quarter-finals of the competition.

This was a country that had never even qualified for a
major tournament and was, by some distance, the smallest
nation to ever come this far. The 30,000-odd Icelanders who
watched their team's stunning victory over the English in
Nice represented nearly ten per cent of the country's population. Back home, they registered a 99.8 per cent rating
on television meaning that, apart from a few hundred
people, everyone was watching the match.

You're not going to find a similar show of unity and
national participation anywhere else in the world, perhaps
not at any time in history. Iceland at the Euros was, at once,
a feel-good story – it was hard not feel affection for these
blue-and-white clad Nordic islanders with their wide-eyed
enthusiasm – and an underdog one: of the twenty-three
men in the squad, just five played in one of Europe's major
leagues and only one, Gylfi Sigurdsson, could be described
as a star.

It was a Cinderella story and, while chance and probability played their part – they always do – this was not a
case of a team riding their luck. For a start, to even get to

the tournament, they had qualified out of a tough group that included former European champions like the Czech Republic and Holland, as well as Turkey, whose population is nearly 300 times greater than Iceland's. At the Euros, they were undefeated in the group stage, finishing ahead of Portugal, led by Cristiano Ronaldo and the eventual winners of the tournament. And evidence that this was no one-time fluke came two years later, when they again qualified for a major tournament: the 2018 World Cup in Russia.

No, Iceland squeezed everything they could out of a tiny population wedged on an inhospitable island with unfavourable conditions for football because they followed a plan. For a start, while this is a tiny nation, it is also one that is obsessed with football. The average crowd at a top division game is just over 1,000. If Germany, a country some 240 times as populous and also football-mad, had a population willing to watch games at the same rate, there would be an average crowd of around a quarter of a million people at every Bundesliga match.

And Icelanders don't just watch football. They play it: one out of every fifteen people on the island is a registered footballer, whether men's, women's or youth. And they don't just play, they learn and they learn from highly qualified coaches. Iceland has 185 coaches who hold the UEFA A coaching licence – that's one for every 1,793 people. Compare that to England, where there's an A-licence coach for every 44,537 people.

Of course, there's no point in having passion for a sport, plenty of people willing to play and outstanding coaches to teach them how, unless you also have the facilities. That's where the 'football house' project comes in. In the late 1990s, Iceland committed to building football facilities across the island so that they could play year-round, even during the unforgiving Arctic winter. These ranged from full-sized indoor pitches to heated outdoor facilities, as well as mini-pitches at virtually every school. There was no excuse. Everyone who wanted to play was able to play, and to do so with proper coaching and pitches.

It wasn't guaranteed – in sport, anything can happen – but what Iceland did was give themselves the best possible chance to succeed, tilting the very steep odds against them as far as they could in their favour. Their reward? An epic Euro adventure to rival the greatest of Nordic sagas. And the memories of that Icelandic 'thunder clap' that stunned the world and was emulated around the globe.

'OBSTACLES ARE CHALLENGES FOR WINNERS AND EXCUSES FOR LOSERS.'

53

WILMA RUDOLPH

Wilma Glodean Rudolph was born in the tiny community of Saint Bethlehem near Clarksville, Tennessee, the twentieth of her father Ed Rudolph's twenty-two children over two marriages.

Everything was stacked against her. She was born premature, weighing around four and a half pounds, and spent most of her childhood in bed as a result of double pneumonia, scarlet fever and, later, polio. When she was six, doctors determined she would never have the use of her left leg, and so Wilma was fitted with metal leg braces.

She would later say she spent most of her early childhood determined to get her braces off. In this endeavour, her many siblings and half-siblings played a critical role. They would take turns massaging her legs, and encouraged her to push herself as far as she could. By the age of nine, she was able to walk unassisted and the braces were later removed.

Her health remained an issue. She contracted first whooping cough, then measles, then chicken pox. But her determination was second to none. After all, she had learned to walk again when everyone said she couldn't. These illnesses weren't going to stop her. Not when she had the loving support of a family that, while poor, was united and determined to see her flourish.

Her first love was basketball, which she played against

her brothers and older boys. She joined the team at the all-African-American Burt High School and soon began to dominate. This earned her the attention of Ed Temple, the athletics coach at Tennessee State University. Wilma was so fast, she could easily be a top sprinter, he thought – except Burt High School didn't have a track and field team. So, Temple convinced the school to start one, mainly so Wilma could learn how to run.

Even while still in high school, Wilma began to train with Tennessee State. She was captivated by Temple, who was neither a professional coach, nor paid for his efforts. Instead, he was a sociology professor, who believed that unity and teamwork were just as critical to achieving success as athletic ability and determination, which Rudolph certainly didn't lack.

She quickly became a media phenomenon, earning a bronze medal at just 16 years of age at the Melbourne Olympics in the 4 x 100 metre relay. She was dubbed the 'Black Gazelle', and newspapers from around the world became captivated with her: the fact that she was extremely humble and attractive, in addition to being lightning-fast, certainly didn't hurt.

Four years later, at the 1960 Olympics in Rome, Rudolph lived up to the hype in every way. She set world records in the 200 metres in the track and field trials before the Games, and in the 4 x 100 metre relay at the Games themselves. She won the 100 metres as well, bringing home three gold medals. Her smile and grace charmed audiences everywhere and, in fact, Temple himself said: 'She has done more for her country than what the United States could have paid her for.'

Yet when she returned home to Tennessee after 1960, she came back to a racially segregated state where Jim Crow laws still ruled. Buford Ellington, the Governor of Tennessee, agreed to arrange a parade and celebration, albeit a segregated one, in keeping with his racist beliefs.

Wilma politely turned him down. She would not be attending any kind of celebration if it was segregated. Ellington relented, and Clarksville held their first deseg-regated banquet and parade in her honour. Her grace and fame were greater than even the power of race politics.

Wilma retired at twenty-two, because she realised ath-letics couldn't provide her with a long-term stable income, despite her fame and success. She became a schoolteacher and later worked for various non-profits. Along the way, she raised four children as a single mother, a remarkable feat, but for her just another challenge, which she took in her stride with her usual determination.

Many female Olympic athletes, particularly athletes of colour, cite her as an inspiration. While flattered, she always politely batted away the compliments: 'There is no comparison. I come from another planet.'

And, given what she'd been through, and what Saint Bethlehem was in the 1950s, she was absolutely right.

'IT'S THE REPETITION
OF AFFIRMATION THAT
LEADS TO BELIEF.
ONCE THAT BELIEF
BECOMES A DEEP
CONVICTION, THINGS
BEGIN TO HAPPEN.'

54

GEORGE 'BABE' RUTH

The Boston Red Sox knew they had something special when, during World War I, a cherubic-faced twenty-year-old named George Ruth joined the Major League Baseball team. What they didn't know was that the kid, soon to be known as 'Babe' and later 'the Bambino' due to his pudgy, child-like features, was exactly what that special something was – and just how special it would be. The upshot was the ultimate double whammy: getting it wrong on two counts. And, possibly, derailing your club for nearly a century.

The Red Sox were a powerhouse who would win four World Series in the 1910s, three of them with Ruth playing a starring role. While he was strong and a good hitter, they saw him primarily as a pitcher – and a very good one at that. In 1916, he led the American League in earned run average and in his first five full seasons he would win eighty-seven games as a pitcher: an impressive tally.

By the end of the 1919 season, however, the Red Sox weren't so sure. Pitching was a specialist position, and the wear and tear on a player's arm meant it was something you could only do every four or five games. But Ruth was a gifted batter as well and, when he wasn't pitching, they tried to get him in the line-up as a hitter, deploying him in the outfield. He led the league in home runs in both 1918 and 1919 (when he hit twenty-nine, breaking the Major

League Record). This made him something of a sensation: a rare player who could both pitch and hit.

Yet deep down, the Red Sox weren't convinced. Baseball had never had a genuine star player who could play both roles effectively. Ruth was neither fish nor fowl. And while his exploits at the bat had garnered plenty of national attention, there was a sense that maybe it was a one-off. After all, the twenty-nine home runs he hit in 1919 made a whopping eighteen more than the eleven he'd hit the year before. Maybe it was a freak occurrence. Maybe his desire to hit out of the park was going to hurt his pitching. And maybe his hitting would suffer if he continued to pitch.

That was the sporting explanation behind the Red Sox's decision to sell Ruth to the New York Yankees for $125,000 in the winter of 1919. He was good – very good – but they just weren't sure what he was, so they opted to cash in. In popular lore, the reason is simple and, perhaps, more romantic. The Red Sox owner, Harry Frazee, was a theatrical producer and needed a quick injection of cash to finance a Broadway musical, *No, No, Nanette*. It's not entirely clear where the truth lies and, even now, more than a century later, we may never know for sure. What's evident, however, is that Frazee viewed the Red Sox as just one part of his entertainment business and had no qualms about using them to finance other branches of his empire.

It would prove to be one of the worst sporting decisions in history. Ruth joined the Yankees and very quickly gave up pitching to focus exclusively on being a hitter. He quickly became one of the greatest in history, winning another ten home-run crowns and a batting title, while leading the Yankees to four World Series titles. In 1927, he hit sixty homes runs, a record that would stand for thirty-four years, and, when he retired in 1935, he had hit a total of 714 – that record would stand until 1974.

Beyond the numbers, Ruth achieved legendary status

as an icon of Americana, and specifically baseball, the national pastime. He was seen as a gentle giant, the Paul Bunyan of the baseball diamond. The adjective 'Ruthian' – to describe something colossal, overpowering and prodigious – entered popular language.

And the Red Sox? They would go eighty-six years without winning a World Series. More than that, they became a sort of byword for suffering and making wrong decisions, a legacy of futility that passed from generation to generation of supporters in what is known as 'Red Sox Nation', the mythical network of fans cursed with a love of the team. Over the years, the mishaps and misfortune mounted, only adding to the lore.

They lost a dramatic World Series in 1946 to the Saint Louis Cardinals, when an opposing player ignored his coach's instruction to stop at third base and instead went on to score the winning run. In 1967, they made another wrong decision, deciding to start the decisive final game of the World Series with Jim Lonborg, a talented pitcher, but one who was clearly fatigued and unwell. In 1975, they blew a 3–0 lead in the final game of the World Series to lose to the Cincinnati Reds. Eleven years later, in 1986, they came to within a single out of beating the New York Mets to finally clinch the World Series, but an error by first baseman Bill Buckner, who allowed the ball to trickle between his legs, led to a dramatic comeback and cost them the title.

Those are just some of the examples: there are more. And as the years wore on, the curse felt more and more real. It finally ended in 2004 and, fittingly, it was as dramatic as the near-misses had been over the decades. The Red Sox advanced to the American League Championship Series – the de facto semi-final – where they faced the hated Yankees (who else?) and found themselves 3–0 down in the best-of-seven series. They were losing the fourth game in the ninth inning when they mounted the most improbable of comebacks, eventually winning the series

4–3 before going on to defeat the Saint Louis Cardinals in the World Series.

The fact that the Cardinals' final batter was Édgar Rentería, who wore number three, the same number Babe Ruth had worn for most of his career, represented a fitting end to the nightmare. The Bambino had been exorcised. The curse was lifted.

'PERFECTION IS NOT
ATTAINABLE BUT IF
WE CHASE PERFECTION
WE WILL CATCH
EXCELLENCE.'

55

NIKI LAUDA

Niki Lauda was born into privilege. For some, that means life is easy, a perpetual downhill ride. For Lauda, while he'd be the first to acknowledge that he enjoyed opportunities others did not, it meant an added layer of responsibility. With gifts this great, failure would hurt him even more. It was down to him to figure out how to make it work: whatever 'it' was.

When he told his parents that 'it' was going to be racing cars, they were strongly opposed. If he was going to go down that route, he'd be doing so on his own dime. They would not be supporting him financially.

This, in some ways, was the least of Lauda's concerns. He'd already had the benefits of an elite education, successful role models in his family and access to contacts and expertise. He'd find the money he needed, and he would find a path. Thus, he dropped out of university, borrowed enough money to buy a Formula Three car and hit the track.

He did well, but not well enough to attract sponsors. Perhaps some were put off by the fact that Lauda's family was so wealthy that, if they wanted to, they could easily back him. So why support a rich kid when there were so many others who needed backing?

So, Lauda doubled down. He had a sizeable life insurance policy and used it to guarantee more loans. This time, he scraped together enough to race in Formula Two, the next step up. Now on a bigger stage, he was noticed almost immediately and was soon in the big-time: Formula One.

Yet he was viewed with some suspicion. He didn't look like a Formula One driver: he didn't have the look or the swagger or the devil-may-care attitude. In fact, he got one of his early nicknames – 'Computer' – precisely because his driving was so calculated. Nothing he did appeared to be based on intuition or gut feeling. Rather, everything – from the distances he kept, to the angles he chose when overtaking – appeared the result of a real-time analytical process in his brain.

His other nickname, which stemmed from members of his own team, is harder to translate: '*Nervensaege*', which literally means 'he who cuts your nerves'. This moniker was based on his obsession with squeezing every possible ounce of performance out of his car, endlessly tinkering with chassis, engine, wheels – every possible component – and often driving his technicians mad with his demands and his prodigious appetite for work.

When Ferrari approached him, he told them he could make the car half a second faster. It seemed like bluster or bragging. But this was Lauda. He didn't boast, and he didn't make promises he couldn't keep. If he said that, he truly believed it. And so, they let him have a go. He worked day and night with the car's engineers and eventually pulled off a lap at the Maranello test track that was 0.8 seconds faster than the year before, with exactly the same chassis and engine (save for Lauda's tinkering and driving).

'I would rather under promise and over deliver,' Lauda said.

He joined Ferrari and won the world title in his second season, 1975. The following year, Lauda was favourite to triumph again, but suffered a horrific accident at the German Grand Prix at Nürburgring, one that would leave him mentally and physically scarred. Lauda had been concerned about the safety measures at the track and had campaigned for a boycott of the race. Failing to garner enough support, he reluctantly raced and, as ever, gave it his all. After his accident, he ended up in a coma and was given the last rites, although he eventually recovered. He was left with extensive scarring to his head and ears, but refused major reconstructive surgery: after all, these were battle scars; this was who he was.

Lauda missed just two races (he was back in the car within six weeks of his accident), and was still favoured to win heading into the final Grand Prix in Japan. On race day, the track was hit by a torrential rainstorm, prompting Lauda to drop out after just two laps. He told Ferrari that the driving conditions were unsafe, and his inability to blink – a result of his earlier accident and damage to his tear ducts – meant he simply couldn't race in those conditions. It would cost him the world title by a single point.

This is where his relationship with the team seriously deteriorated, particularly as they put out their own version of why he retired from the race, blaming faulty electrics in the car. This upset Lauda greatly. He had a reason for retiring from the race, it was a valid reason, and he wasn't going to be 'macho' about it or blame somebody else. There was no need for the team to 'protect' him.

Still, he won another world title in 1977, having already decided to leave Ferrari at the end of that season. He raced for two more years at another team, Brabham, then retired, founding a charter airline, Lauda Air.

In 1982, however, he returned to Formula One, this time driving for McLaren. Many thought he was finished, and that this was just a publicity stunt, especially when the team hired the young French prodigy Alain Prost to race their other car. It looked as if Lauda would, at best, be serving as Prost's mentor.

Instead, the pair went head-to-head throughout the 1984 season. At one point, Lauda said: 'Prost and I have exactly the same car, exactly the same team behind us and exactly the same level of talent. If I'm going to win this, I'm going to need to be smarter and figure it out.'

And that's what he did. He ended up winning his third world title by the slimmest of margins, just half a point, something made possible when the authorities stopped the Monaco Grand Prix halfway through, due to bad weather, and simply awarded half the usual points for the race. The calculating 'Computer' had lived up to his name and had squeezed through by a wafer-thin margin once again.

'DIE WITH MEMORIES,
NOT DREAMS.'

56

PATRICK DE GAYARDON

We associate extreme sports with recklessness. They go hand-in-hand, whether it's snowboarders on moguls or free runners doing parkour across rooftops. These are people with a different appetite for risk. Some might even say they have a death wish. But the man who, in some ways, started it all, Patrick De Gayardon, was rather different.

He once turned down the opportunity to do some bungee jumping. 'It's not something I'd ever do unless I brought my own cord,' he explained. That's what extreme sport was for him: challenging yourself and taking risks, but always calculated ones. Calculated right down to the nth degree, in fact. Leaping off a mountainside with someone else's bungee cord, without knowing what condition it was in, how many jumps it had been involved in, what weight it could hold . . . no. Not for him.

And yet this was a guy brave enough to base jump out of a helicopter and down the Sótano de las Golondrinas (the 'Cave of Swallows'), a natural canyon in Mexico some 376 metres deep and no more than fifty metres wide, knowing that he could not open his parachute until he was well inside the canyon. Which, of course, was as black as night.

But for him, it was all about timing and comfort. Timing was all about when to jump, when to move in the air, when to open the ripcord on his parachute. He could discipline himself to get that right. And as for comfort, few men in history have been as comfortable as he was free-falling in the air. Where others might panic or lose their orientation, his became narrowly focused. It was almost as if this was his natural state.

De Gayardon basically invented 'skysurfing' in his mid-twenties, jumping out of airplanes with a snowboard on his feet and effectively 'riding' the air. He was moving vertically downwards, yes, but also horizontally. The idea of travelling across both the x-axis and y-axis with no support sounds terrifying, but he was born to do this.

The next logical evolution from there was winged flight: creating a body suit with material under the arms that would replicate the wings of a bird or an airplane. It's not a new concept. Leonardo da Vinci had explored such ideas hundreds of years earlier, and in 1912 a man named Franz Reichelt fell to his death after jumping off the Eiffel Tower wearing what he dubbed a 'parachute suit'.

De Gayardon found his inspiration in nature, studying the sugar glider (*Petaurus breviceps*), a nocturnal possum whose loose skin enables it to glide through the air. He designed his suit with special material between the legs and under each arm. And off he went, becoming the first human being to fly without mechanical support.

He mastered the wing suit to the point that the speed at which he dropped to earth – around fifty miles an hour – was substantially less than his forward, gliding speed, which reached 120 miles an hour, with a drop angle of around thirty-five degrees. He was literally flying, covering huge amounts of ground: as much as five or six miles in a single jump.

It wasn't magic. It was the ingenuity of the human brain, combined with the courage of the human spirit, along with the fact that this particular human was blessed with superb body control and nerves of steel.

De Gayardon died while jumping in 1998 after both his main parachute and his back-up failed to open. Sheer, tragic misfortune. Despite the thousand checks he might have made before boarding that airplane, ultimately there were things beyond his control.

But he had shown it could be done. He had broken the barrier, 'slipped the surly bonds of earth' and taken to the air, paving the way for others to follow. And it was anything but reckless.

'DON'T LET SOMEONE
GET COMFORTABLE
DISRESPECTING YOU.'

57

BIBIANA STEINHAUS

The world may be changing – I might say evolving – but there are some professions which remain nearly impermeable and impregnable to women. Coaching or officiating men's football are among them. The pace of change may be slow, but there are trailblazers. One of them is Bibiana Steinhaus who, in 2017, became the first woman to referee a top-flight men's game in one of Europe's 'Big Five' leagues.

'I don't feel like a pioneer,' she told the *New York Times*. 'For me, this is normality. And I wish it were so for everyone.'

Except it isn't. Because even someone like Steinhaus had to wait for her chance. This despite the fact that she's the daughter of a referee, that she became a qualified match official at the age of fifteen and that she scaled her way up from the lowest rung. Oh, and she's also a police officer in her day job, which – while obviously not a prerequisite for becoming a referee – is no doubt beneficial when it comes to keeping order on the pitch.

It took her twenty-three years from her debut at the age of fifteen to get her shot at the top. Along the way, she alternated lower-league men's games with top-flight women's games. Obviously, in the women's game, her path was more straightforward and, in fact, she was chosen to officiate the 2011 Women's World Cup Final.

She's had her knocks along the way, like every referee. Footballers are, in the main, young men filled with testosterone, and when they don't get their own way, they're not shy about letting their feelings be known. The difference is that when you're a female referee, your gender is used as an insult.

Like when Kerem Demirbay, a midfielder for Fortuna Düsseldorf, fumed that 'women have f***-all to do with football' after she sent him off for a second bookable offence. Demirbay later called her to apologise; that did not stop the German FA from slapping him with a five-game ban. Though, perhaps, more effective than that in changing his attitude was the second part of his punishment: being sent to referee a junior girls' game.

Then there was the time when, in a different kind of sexism, the Iranian state broadcaster effectively chose to edit her out of the clash between Cologne and Bayern Munich. She was picked to officiate the game and, to most viewers around the world, that's what she did. But those in Iran saw a different match. Every close-up of Steinhaus was replaced with random shots of the crowd or replays of events minutes earlier. You can just make her out in some shots, but only from a distance, and you wouldn't know it was her from that far away.

She took it in her stride, just like she took every other step of her career. We may still have a long way to go when it comes to women in football, but there is no question that we have passed the point of no return. And there's no going back.

That is what makes Steinhaus the sort of trailblazer that others can follow.

'IF SIZE MATTERED
THE ELEPHANT
WOULD BE THE
KING OF THE JUNGLE!'

58

TYRONE BOGUES

Being short is not necessarily a hurdle, depending on your sport. Heck, it never slowed down Lionel Messi. But imagine being a full ten centimetres smaller than Messi. And playing the sort of sport where the goal isn't right there at eye level, but three metres up in the air.

Tyrone 'Muggsy' Bogues didn't spend much time thinking about his height: five feet, three inches. Growing up in Baltimore's tough Lafayette Court public housing project, with his father in prison, he had other things to worry about. One of them was basketball. His body was no doubt a hurdle if he just thought about playing the traditional way. But his size also brought advantages – plenty of them. Being small in stature gave him a speed that made him tough to catch, a dribble so low to the hardwood floor it was nearly impossible to take the ball from him, and passing angles that were beyond the reach of taller men.

Of course, he was also blessed with natural gifts, like the ability not to just see passes and movement, but to anticipate them. But this would have all been meaningless without a ferocious work ethic that ensured his body, while small, was packed with muscle and strength, necessary qualities to enable him to hold his ground against bigger opponents.

Bogues stood out on the Baltimore playgrounds from a young age and was recruited to play at Dunbar High

School, a city powerhouse. There, he starred on one of the finest high school teams ever assembled, alongside three future NBA stars David Wingate, Reggie Williams and Reggie Lewis. In fact, it speaks volumes about the strength of that team that Lewis, a future NBA All-star and captain of the Boston Celtics, came off the bench in his senior season.

It wasn't all smooth sailing, at least at first. Because while Dunbar had a nationwide reputation, when they travelled out of state, the sight of a player Tyrone's size sometimes drew howls of derision from opposing fans, who didn't quite realise what was about to be unleashed on them. It happened when Dunbar drove north to New Jersey, to take on Camden High, led by Billy Thompson, considered the number-one high school player in the country. The crowd laughed at Bogues and called him 'water boy' during the warm up. It got so bad that the Dunbar coach asked Bogues if he was OK.

'Coach, I'm about to have a party,' he replied, before flashing that toothy grin. Dunbar went on to win by twenty-five points.

Still, when it was time to move on to college, opinion was split. Most coaches could appreciate his skills, but just weren't sure they would translate at the next level. The coaches argued it was relatively easy to look good as a point guard when you have such gifted teammates to pass to and your team was so dominant. But what would happen when Bogues faced opponents who could match his speed, while also being several inches taller?

Maybe that's why he only got two offers. One was from Georgetown, one of the best teams in the country, but it felt as if maybe they were doing him a favour. One of his teammates, Wingate, had gone there the year before and another, Williams, had accepted their offer for the following season. It felt to some as if they were looking for a 'package': that Wingate and Williams were the ones they really wanted and Bogues – who was very popular with teammates and fans – was along for the ride. What's more, Georgetown already had a talented point guard, Michael Jackson, who was just a year older than Bogues.

Georgetown represented an opportunity to play for a national contender, alongside two former teammates he had known since childhood, less than an hour from his house. But Bogues wanted to be outside his comfort zone, so he took the other offer he received, from Wake Forest. He was going to move all the way to North Carolina.

Those who advised against it – and there were many among his friends and family – appeared to be proved right in his first two seasons. So too did those who felt that his achievements at Dunbar were all well and good, but this was big-time college basketball and no place for little guys. Bogues hardly got off the bench for two years and considered transferring elsewhere, to a lesser school. But then a new coach, Bob Staak, arrived in town. Amid general scepticism, Staak gave Bogues the starting job. During his final two years of college, Wake Forest improved tremendously and Bogues made his mark on the court, leaving university as the all-time career leader in steals and assists in the Atlantic Coast Conference, one of the top university leagues. Along the way, Wake Forest retired his number 14 jersey and he was selected for the US national team, who won the 1986 World Championships.

Now it was time to move up another level, to the NBA. Enter all the familiar questions and scepticism. When Washington picked him in the first round, it was suggested in some quarters that the move was all about selling tickets, but perhaps this didn't just apply to Bogues: Washington also featured Manute Bol, who, at seven feet, seven inches, was the tallest player in the history of the league. In fact, the two were regularly depicted together on magazine covers and promotional material as a sort of 'small and tall' combination.

After just one season, Bogues moved to the newly formed Charlotte Hornets, where he silenced the doubters once and for all. Over the next decade, he transformed the fledgling side into a perennial contender. He's still their all-time leader in minutes played, assists and steals.

Those fourteen seasons in the NBA left little doubt: it's not about the size of the dog in the fight, it's about the size of the fight in the dog.

He retired with these words: 'Others always judged me on my height. I get that. When people don't know you, they judge you based on how you appear. It's up to you to show them what you can do and have them judge you on that.'

'ONE FINDS LIMITS BY PUSHING THEM.'

59

SERGEY BUBKA

By this stage, you've probably realised that many of these stories feature determined athletes with a laser-like focus on the prize. Well, Sergey Bubka may have been the most determined of all. Tales of his work ethic stretch back to his youth.

As a child growing up in what is now Luhansk in eastern Ukraine, he'd often opt to train, usually by himself, rather than going off to play with friends. Back then, he was a sprinter and a long jumper: the pole vault was not yet on his radar.

In his early twenties, just as his contemporaries were getting into style and fashion, Bubka was notorious for wearing oversized clothes, his outfits often cobbled together without any care. It was as if he simply reached into his wardrobe and grabbed whatever was there: trousers, shirt, jumper . . . off you go. And they were baggy because that made them comfortable. It was the same with his hair: always the same short bowl cut. Easy, fast, convenient.

By that stage, Bubka had devoted his life to pole vaulting. It's a discipline that requires a unique blend of speed, strength, nerves and, perhaps above all, coordination and body control. His progression once he hit the world stage was nothing short of staggering.

He set his first world record at the age of twenty, broke it a week later, then broke it again a month later. Six weeks after that – you guessed it! – he broke it once more. A year later, he sailed past it yet again, reaching a height of six metres – something which had previously been considered beyond the reach of human beings.

Between 1984 and 1988 he would break his own world record no fewer than nine times, improving the mark by twenty centimetres in just four years. There's arguably no record in any discipline that has ever been improved so many times – and so substantially – over such a short period.

Bubka didn't stop there. He continued breaking records right through to 1994, when he reached a height of six metres and fourteen centimetres. It wasn't lost on anyone that his last ten world records improved on the previous ones by a single centimetre each time. This gave rise to the popular notion that Bubka was careful not to push too hard, but rather improved his own mark by the smallest possible margin each time. Why? Well, supposedly because in the old Soviet Union, athletes received substantial prizes if they set world records. This, people claimed, was his way of doing it step by step, without 'wasting' potential prize money.

That story is only partially true. A better reading would be that Bubka was the ultimate perfectionist, obsessed with incremental success achieved by tiny tweaks. He experimented with longer poles and more rigid poles, and worked on a different technique for vaulting rather than the traditional technique of simply trying to achieve maximum bend on the pole.

He gave very few interviews, but when he did speak out, he offered a very cogent explanation for his relentlessness.

He said he believed it was an athlete's job to seduce people, and that there was only one measuring stick for success. He noted that athletes have a very short shelf life, that every moment – in training and competition – has to count. He pointed out that nothing happens by chance. For him, everything was incremental. Each competitive record he broke was a record he had already broken in training. He knew it was possible.

Bubka's record stood for some twenty years. It was broken in 2014 by Renaud Lavillenie and, ironically, it happened in Donetsk, just a short drive from where Bubka was born and raised. Bubka was there that day and, for once, betrayed emotion when his record was broken.

'How do I feel? Proud, above all,' he said. 'Lavillenie is an athlete who wants to push the boundaries of what is possible and works relentlessly to do so. I couldn't think of a better heir to my world record.'

'THE FIRST STEP
TOWARDS CHANGE IS
TO BECOME AWARE OF
YOUR OWN BULLSHIT.'

60

MARK McGWIRE

It took Mark McGwire a long time to come clean.

He was one of the greatest home-run hitters in baseball history. He won a World Series with the Oakland Athletics in 1989 and shattered Roger Maris's single-season home run record – one that many felt would never be broken – by hitting seventy home runs in 1998. When he retired, in 2001, he had the fifth highest number of home runs of all time. Those ahead him in the list – Frank Robinson, Willie Mays, Babe Ruth and Hank Aaron – read like a *Who's Who* of baseball lore.

And yet there was a cloud over that era in baseball. Rumours that something was going on – from the use of 'juiced' balls that flew further to widespread performance-enhancing drug use – were rife. Players were hitting home runs at a clip never seen before. It wasn't just McGwire. Even hitting just fifty home runs in a season was traditionally considered a herculean feat. Until 1994, it had been achieved nineteen times in the century-long history of the sport. That is the same number of times as it occurred between 1994 and 2006, when tougher rules regulating the use of steroids came into effect,

In 1998, at the height of the home-run boom – the season that would see McGwire hit seventy and three other players surpass the fifty mark – McGwire told a reporter from the Associated Press that he took androstenedione, a muscle enhancement product. At the time it was banned by the World Anti-Doping Agency and the International Olympic Committee, but not, crucially, by Major League Baseball.

His admission stirred up a hornets' nest of investigative reporters determined to get to the truth, and it put pressure on the baseball authorities. Androstenedione wasn't illegal, sure, and you could buy it over the counter, but clearly if players were taking it and getting such instant improvement, it required a long, hard look.

It wasn't McGwire's intent to ratchet up scrutiny. As he saw it, he simply answered a question and moved on. He refused the role of whistle-blower even after he retired in 2001. He saw himself as a baseball player and nothing more, and players had closed ranks.

In 2005, his former teammate Jose Canseco wrote a controversial autobiography in which he claimed he personally injected McGwire with steroids, a charge McGwire did not concede. The government opened a congressional investigation in which they were both called to testify, during which McGwire broke down in tears.

'Asking me or any other player to answer questions about who took steroids in front of television cameras will not solve the problem,' he said. 'If a player answers no, he simply will not be believed; if he answers yes, he risks public scorn and endless government investigation.'

On the advice of his lawyers, he added, he refused to answer further on the grounds that it might jeopardise himself, his family or his friends.

That day would haunt McGwire for another five years. Many who had regarded him as a hero now viewed him as a cheat who had hidden behind legalese and technicalities. And because this was baseball, it mattered more. In the United States, baseball is not just another sport: it's the national pastime. It's revered, if not downright sacred.

But in 2010, he finally unburdened himself.

'I wish I had never touched steroids,' he said. 'It was foolish and it was a mistake. I truly apologise.' He admitted using them at various stages in his career, including during his record-breaking 1998 campaign. It was an admission that many of his peers refused to make.

And when, a few years later, he won the World Series as an assistant coach with the St Louis Cardinals, he received a standing ovation from the crowd – not because of his role in the victory, but because baseball, and those who love it, had forgiven him.

'CONFUSE THEM WITH SILENCE. AMAZE THEM WITH ACTION.'

61

MARK EDMONDSON

Mark Edmondson was a tall, lanky Aussie with a shock of wild, dark hair and a big handlebar moustache. It was 1976 and the twenty-two-year-old certainly looked the part. While technically he was a professional tennis player, it certainly didn't pay the bills.

He was ranked 212th in the world and made ends meet as a handyman, doing odd jobs like cleaning windows and floors in his native Gosford, in New South Wales. Whatever prize money he earned playing tennis was a cherry on top, not something to be counted on. He was OK with that, even though when he was younger, he had been considered a major prospect (and was even coached by Charlie Hollis, who had worked with the legendary Rod Laver).

Ten days before the start of the Australian Open – a tournament which, at best, Edmondson had imagined he'd watch on television – he received a phone call from the organisers. There was a spot available in the Tasmanian Open and they could get him a wild card. The Tasmanian Open offered a lucky few the chance to qualify for the Australian Open, but that was the furthest thing from his mind at the time. Instead, he figured he'd take a trip down to Tasmania and have some fun playing for a few days.

To everyone's surprise, Edmondson won the Tasmanian Open, earning a spot at the Australian Open at the Kooyong

Lawn Tennis Club in Melbourne. He was under no illusions, but figured this might be his one and only chance to play at Kooyong. Despite having won the prize money from the Tasmanian Open, he didn't want to overstretch his budget, so rather than staying at the official players' hotel, the Hilton, Edmondson bunked down at a friend's house, taking the tram to the Open each day. It was just under an hour there and just under an hour back.

Although that year's Australian Open didn't feature some of the world's top players – Björn Borg, Jimmy Connors, Illie Năstase and Guillermo Vilas all stayed home – it was still a very tough field, with the likes of Ken Rosewall and defending champion John Newcombe.

Edmondson struggled past his first opponent in five sets, then upset the fifth seed, Phil Dent, in the second round. He won again, advancing to the quarter-finals, where he faced Dick Crealy. This was the first time that Edmondson got to step on to one of the main courts. As he was walking around it on the morning of the match, he bumped into Newcombe.

'Kid, how well do you know this court?' the defending champion asked him.

'Not at all. I've only played on court twenty-seven, in front of three men and a dog . . .' Edmondson replied.

So Newcombe gave him some pointers, flagging up dead spots on the court and offering up various pieces of advice. Little did he know that he and Edmondson would meet again.

For Crealy was dispatched a few hours later, setting up a semi-final for Edmondson against crowd favourite Rosewall. Rosewall was now in his forties and had first won the Australian Open back in 1953, before Edmondson was even born. He knew this tournament better than anyone and was the overwhelming favourite.

Yet against all odds, Edmondson prevailed in four sets, winning a place in the final against the heavily favoured

Newcombe. On the tram, travelling to and from the Open, he was now getting recognised by well-wishers. Everyone was friendly, but everyone agreed that he had no chance. The only thing he and Newcombe had in common was a moustache.

The day of the final was hot and windy. So windy, in fact, that the match had to be suspended for half an hour during the first set, which Newcombe won on a tie-break. But it was clear that Newcombe's rhythm was off that day, whether due to the wind or simply his opponent's date with destiny. Edmondson roared back to win the second and third sets. The wind evidently affected the game, but for whatever reason, it seemed to hurt Newcombe more. Edmondson won in the most dramatic fashion, when Newcombe's ball hit the tape at the top of the net and then appeared to be pushed back by a gust of wind.

Incredible as it sounds, the 212th ranked player in the world won the Australian Open. It's a record that stands to this day. Nobody ranked anywhere near as low has ever won a Grand Slam.

Edmondson was totally unprepared. In fact, not only did he drop the trophy on the winners' podium, he followed it up with an audible expletive, which only made him more likeable to the crowd. He took the tram home with the trophy on his lap and the prize money cheque in his pocket. Just another day of the impossible becoming reality in sport.

'PAIN MAKES YOU STRONGER, TEARS MAKE YOU BRAVER, HEARTBREAK MAKES YOU WISER. BE GRATEFUL FOR YOUR PAST BECAUSE IT HELPED SHAPE WHO YOU ARE. AND SO THANK THE PAST FOR A BETTER FUTURE.'

62

SERENA WILLIAMS

Serena Williams spent her early years in Compton, a Los Angeles neighbourhood perhaps made most famous by the gangsta rap group NWA in the late 1980s. Yet, in many ways, she was kept away from the rough world around her thanks to the single-mindedness of her father, Richard. From a very early age she and her older sister, Venus, were put through daily rigorous tennis training sessions, and they soon made a name for themselves on the youth circuit.

The two sisters were a year apart in age, but physically different. Many felt Venus was more suited to tennis: she was taller, longer-limbed, more athletic. Both hit the ball with great power and accuracy, but to many Venus simply 'looked' like more of a tennis player.

As it happened, they would be wrong. Both women would reach number one in the world, but Serena would arguably achieve more. She won the US Open at eighteen and, four years later, won all four Grand Slam tournaments in succession.

In September 2003, a few months after winning her second consecutive Wimbledon title, she was in Toronto, recovering from an injury that had kept her out of the US Open. As she often did, she chatted on the phone with her older half-sister, Yetunde, with whom she was especially close. A few hours later, she received the news that Yetunde was dead, shot along with her boyfriend in a gang-related drive-by shooting in Los Angeles.

It hit Serena very hard. In the words of Serena and Venus, 'she was our nucleus and our rock'. Serena reacted to this loss in the way she'd been told to react: focus on tennis, focus on rehab, throw yourself into your work. It's therapeutic, supposedly.

But even when she returned to full fitness the following spring, Serena had hit a wall. Her dominance of the Grand Slam tournaments was a thing of the past. A young Maria Sharapova dispatched her with ease in the 2004 Wimbledon final. That and the 2005 Australian Open would be her only Grand Slam finals in more than three years. Some questioned her desire and whether she had fallen out of love with the game. Few thought she would ever be the same.

She was beset by injuries – her knee, her ankle – but, as she would later reveal, things ran much deeper than that. Serena took several months off in 2006, even as her ranking slid out of the top ten, then the top fifty, then right down into the eighties. The truth was, she was battling depression. And one of the key things that helped her out of it was one of several trips she took to Africa.

She travelled to Gorée Island, just off the coast of Senegal, in November of 2006. Serena stood at what is known as 'the Door of No Return', the gate through which African men, women and children passed before being shipped off as slaves to the Americas and the Caribbean.

'All you see is the Atlantic Ocean,' she would later say. 'It was just mind-boggling to think about what my ancestors went through. That just changed me. It gave me strength and courage and it let me know that I can endure anything.' For Serena, it was a turning point. She returned 'as a different person'.

Her next Grand Slam, in January 2007, was the Australian Open. She was out of shape but still managed to cruise to the final, where she demolished none other than Sharapova, exacting a measure of revenge for her Wimbledon defeat two years earlier.

That victory was all about guts and desire. It took a little while for Serena to regain her game shape and take her tennis back to the level it had been. But when she did, she was once again uber-dominant. In the decade between 2008 and 2017, when she took time off after having a child, she won four Australian Opens, two French Opens, four US Opens and five Wimbledon titles.

Her mind was clear. Her journey was complete. And she was once again the Queen of Tennis.

'THE EXPERT IN EVERYTHING ONCE WAS A BEGINNER!'

63

TORBEN GRAEL

Sometimes, it's in the blood. But you still have to buckle down and make it happen.

Torben Grael was five years old when his grandfather took him to sea on a boat that looked like an antique. It was the *Aileen* and it had a glorious history: it was the sailing boat the Danish team had used to capture the silver medal in the six-metre category at the 1912 Summer Olympics in Stockholm, fifty-four years earlier.

Torben was smitten. The wind, the sea, the sails . . . he knew this was what he wanted to do. Growing up in Niterói, just across the Guanabara Bay from Rio de Janeiro, the water was always nearby, but it wasn't until he was thirteen that he was able to go out there on his own. He started out at the lowest rung of sailing with a Laser, a small dinghy.

Even as he learned to master the waves and the winds, he wanted more, so he volunteered to help his uncles. Erik and Axel were twins, who, like most of his family, had the sailing bug. In fact, they were known in sailing circles as the 'sea twins' and they competed at the Pan American Games and Olympics. The uncles were competitive and, at first, they weren't sure about having their young nephew hanging around while they tried to train. But sponsorship money was thin on the ground and, while they were solidly middle class, sailing was expensive. An extra pair of hands was useful.

And so young Torben got to work, carrying out the most menial of tasks around the boat. But what all that washing, waxing and rigging did was teach him about every minor detail. It helped him discover that, as Torben himself would later say: 'Water can make you do amazing things . . . you just have to be near it.'

As luck would have it, the 1978 Soling World Championships were to be held in Rio de Janeiro. The twins weren't sure about entering: they usually competed on different boats. But Torben, who had just turned seventeen, insisted that they participate.

With a bit of reluctance – and knowing that they had plenty of time to pull out if they couldn't prepare properly or secure the funding – they agreed. One problem: they didn't have a boat that conformed to the requirements of Soling class, and it wasn't clear how they could get one. Torben scoured the harbours and boat sales in and around Rio de Janeiro. One day, he found an old fishing boat. With the right modifications, he said, they could turn it into a Soling keelboat.

Axel and Erik were sceptical. But, to be fair, by this point their teenage nephew probably knew as much – if not more – than they did about the actual structure of sailing boats, given the amount of time he spent working on them. And so, after a lot of work, they took the Soling out at the World Championships. They expected a calm, fun regatta, figuring there was no way they could compete against state-of-the-art custom-made Solings sailed by people who had far more experience with them than they did.

They were wrong.

The pair finished tenth, shocking the field. While they received praise, they knew that it would never have happened without Torben's modifications to the boat. From that moment, they basically turned over their dinghies and keelboats to him, telling him that he had proven himself to be the greater sailor. Just a few months later, Torben competed in the World Championships in San Diego, finishing first in the Snipe Junior class. He would go on to win numerous titles, as well as five Olympic medals – two golds, one silver and two bronze – spread over five editions of the games, from Los Angeles in 1984 to Athens in 2004. No Olympic sailor has won more.

The tradition continues. His daughter, Martine, won Olympic gold in 2016 in the 49er FX class. To make it sweeter, she did it right there in Rio de Janeiro, in Guanabara Bay, where her father, grandfather and great uncles had sailed.

'IT'S NOT THE LOAD THAT BREAKS YOU DOWN, IT'S THE WAY YOU CARRY IT.'

64

DON BRADMAN

Don Bradman is a name synonymous with batting excellence in cricket. In fact, a popular saying at the peak of his career was this: 'Bradman isn't an Australian batsman. He's three Australian batsmen.' Why? Because he single-handedly scored as many runs as three or four – sometimes more – 'ordinary' cricketers.

Bradman retired with a batting average of 99.94 in Test cricket. Nobody else in the venerable history of the game has an average higher than sixty-four (among those who have appeared in at least twenty Tests). Bradman's average is not just a mind-boggling number: it's almost as if it belonged to an entirely different sport.

In his heyday – the 1930s and 1940s – he was the most famous cricketer in the world, a superstar who drew thronging crowds everywhere he went. Yet he was also extremely down-to-earth and a devoted family man. He and his wife Jessie, who he met when she boarded with his family while at school, lived for almost their entire lives in a modest, unremarkable suburban house in Adelaide. It was almost as if because what he did on the cricket pitch was so extraordinary, remaining as ordinary as possible in his private life was an absolute priority.

Sadly, Bradman's family life was harshly tested. His first son died as an infant. His second, John, contracted polio. His daughter, Shirley, had cerebral palsy from birth. At the peak of his career, Bradman himself nearly died after suffering from an acute appendicitis attack, exacerbated by peritonitis.

His popularity and status as a folk hero were so overwhelming that his son John struggled to cope with the pressures of being a Bradman. John legally changed his last name to 'Bradsen' in 1972, when he was in his early thirties.

It was a blow for Don. He and John drifted apart over the years. This was partly because, by that stage, Don's wife Jessie was in poor health following open-heart surgery. Don became more and more reclusive, avoiding public appearances and devoting most of his time to caring for Jessie.

In 1997, Jessie passed away at the age of eighty-eight, a victim of cancer. Don sunk into depression and grieving. But one day – in what may be an apocryphal story – there was a knock at the door.

'Go away, I don't want to talk to anyone!' Don called, without getting out of the chair in his living room.

'It's me, John,' was the reply.

'I don't know anyone named John!'

'It's, me, Dad. John Bradman.'

It was the critical first step towards a reconciliation that would see John take on an active role in Don's final years. John become a spokesperson for the family and helped ensure that his father's name and legacy would remain valued. The name Bradman is still synonymous with excellence and class, and John made sure he lived up to it in the final years of his father's life and beyond.

'YOUR LOVE MAKES ME STRONG; YOUR HATE MAKES ME UNSTOPPABLE.'

65

HASSIBA BOULMERKA

Ever since she was ten years old, Hassiba Boulmerka had raced through the dusty streets and over the picturesque bridges of Constantine, an Algerian city high up on the plateau, cut through by a dramatic deep ravine. As a child, her running was cute; as an adolescent, it became controversial. Because, while Constantine is a modern, prosperous city, the sight of a young woman – bare arms and legs, large shock of jet-black hair – running on her own by the side of the road made many uncomfortable.

This was the 1980s. Algeria was an Islamic country, and this was a place where change came slowly. Hassiba would regularly receive insults, dirty looks, sometimes even threats. Believing she'd be better off in the countryside, running along the agricultural lanes, or in the foothills of the Atlas Mountains, scrambling up the rocky trails, she went further afield. Except while she now encountered fewer people, those she did meet were less tolerant and more aggressive. A shepherd with a flock of goats who suddenly came face to face with a teenage girl in a tank top and shorts, dark hair flapping in the wind, would not often react well. Hassiba was spat at, chased away with rocks, and told she would rot in hell.

Her parents, who had supported her when she was younger, asked her to stop once they realised what she faced every day. They admired her single-mindedness and work ethic, they shared her desire to break barriers, but not at the expense of their little girl's well-being.

But, still, she ran. And ran some more. She ran up steep ravines and down rocky hills. She didn't run away from insults and mockery. She ran through them and came out the other side.

Then, in 1991, at the Athletics World Championships in Tokyo, Hassiba's story went from local to global. She outpaced the reigning World Champion, Tetyana Dorovskikh, in a furious sprint in the final half-lap that saw her accelerate away from the pack. Afterwards, Hassiba said: 'This is for all the Algerian women, all the women in the Arab world.'

At once she became a heroine and an inspiration to some, while being seen as a dangerous public enemy by others. Thousands gathered at Algiers airport to hail her return home, even as a fundamentalist political party, the Islamic Salvation Front, was sweeping to power in local elections. To their traditionalist supporters, Hassiba was a symbol of all that was going wrong with Algeria. Some called for her to be put to death.

'It was Friday prayers at our local mosque and the Imam said that I was not a Muslim because I had run in shorts, I had shown my legs,' she would later recall. 'He said I was anti-Muslim.' The country soon broke into civil war, and the threats against Hassiba intensified. She was forced to move to Berlin in order to train safely for the 1992 Olympics in Barcelona. That meant severing ties with her family as well, since they too had become targets for the fundamentalists. The situation disintegrated, and she ended up traveling to Spain via Oslo, in secret, escorted everywhere by armed guards. The International Olympic Committee tried to persuade her to cover her shoulders, hair and legs to appease her critics. It was a question of diplomacy, they said. But she was having none of it. Apart from wearing shorts rather than a singlet, she would race dressed exactly like the others.

She won the Women's 1500 metres, once again coming from behind in the final half-lap, powering into the lead before turning on the turbo, as if powered by all the women in the Arab world who were willing her to make history.

After the finish, she thrust one arm out, like an archer, and slowly raised her other, fist clenched, face beaming with confidence.

'It was a symbol of defiance,' she would later say. 'It was my way of saying, "I did it! I won! And now, if you kill me, it will be too late. I've made history!"'

History had indeed been made. Nothing would ever be the same again.

'PRAY AS IF IT'S DOWN TO GOD BUT WORK AS IF IT'S UP TO YOU.'

66

WAYNE GRETZKY

'Jesus saves . . . but Gretzky scores on the rebound!' The fact that such a phrase could become a running joke in North America tells you a lot about the high regard in which Wayne Gretzky is held. So, too, does his nickname: 'The Great One'.

In ice hockey, a sport that can sometimes be dominated by brawny bruisers ready to throw you into the boards or drop gloves and have a punch-up, Gretzky stood out. Not for his physical prowess (he was six feet tall and weighed seventy-two kilograms when he entered the National Hockey League, nearly fourteen kilograms less than the average player), nor his athletic gifts (he was by no means slow, but not particularly fast either), but rather because he seemed to be the ultimate manipulator of time and space, as if he knew where the puck was going to go before everybody else.

Even if you're not a hockey fan, you will know what we're talking about here. There are great players in team sports who always look as if there is nobody close to them, as if they have oodles of time on the ball. That was Gretzky. He created space and time for himself, which, on a small surface like a hockey rink, is particularly hard to do.

Here are some numbers to put his career achievements in context. He won the Hart Trophy, the award for the most valuable player in the league, nine times in the twenty seasons that he played in the NHL (eight of these were in a row). He is the only player in history to have recorded 200 or more points (goals plus assists) in a single season – and he did it four times. He is the all-time leader in both goals (894) and assists (1963). For context, only seven other players have 700 or more goals, and the man who ranks second for all-time assists has 1,249. Along the way, Gretzky won the Stanley Cup, the NHL championship, four times. And when he was traded from the Edmonton Oilers, a small team in northern Canada, to the Los Angeles Kings, there were calls in the Canadian parliament for the deal to be blocked.

Gretzky's ability to anticipate was spoken of in hushed terms in hockey circles. It almost seemed to rankle that this relatively small man without evident physical attributes could so dominate the game, and many spoke of an innate 'sixth sense' – like echolocation in bats – that allowed him to seemingly know ahead of time what was going to happen.

Gretzky always disputed it. And when he revealed the 'secret' of his success, it was far more romantic than supernatural. It was simply the result of hours and hours practising with his dad, Wally. In winter, his backyard could be flooded and turned into an ice rink. Indeed, that's why Wally had bought the house: because the yard was big enough and flat enough for this purpose.

Wally devised many of the drills himself, using improvised items. Today, these drills form part of any ice hockey education, but back then he was probably the only person in North America doing them. Wally would lay down plastic bottles and use them as cones to ensure that Wayne skated in a tight, controlled way. There were drills where Wayne would have to pick up the puck off the ice and on to his stick while going at full speed: a skill that seemed pointless to some, but which gave him an incredibly refined stick-handling ability.

As for the anticipation, Wally drilled certain basic mantras into Wayne's head, which, when reading them here, might seem obvious. 'The last place a player looks when he's passing is to the guy he's passing to . . . so get over there and intercept it.' 'Always skate to where the puck is going, not to where it is or where it's been.'

Gretzky himself said that what appeared to be some kind of natural instinct was, in fact, simply the result of years of practice and study. 'Nobody would ever say a doctor had learned his profession by instinct; yet, in my own way, I've put in almost as much time studying hockey as a medical student puts in studying medicine.'

The legend of Gretzky will live on for years to come, and it's unlikely his records will ever be broken. That anticipation, that ability to effectively predict the immediate future outshone his other gifts in some ways, and that's unfortunate. Because Gretzky was also a natural leader, ice-cool under pressure and possessed of a work ethic that was second to none. As for his God-given talent, well, let's just say that, if that was all he had, he would have been 'one of the great ones' rather than, indisputably, 'The Great One'.

'NO MATTER HOW MUCH WEALTH AND SUCCESS COMES YOUR WAY ALWAYS STAY HUMBLE.'

67

DJALMA SANTOS

It's not what you expect from a two-time World Cup winner. Or maybe it is. Or, at least, maybe it should be.

In 1985, the Brazilian manager Chinesinho agreed to coach Bassano, a small club in the Veneto region, an hour or so from Venice. He had been a decent striker in his day, capped for his country, and had even enjoyed spells at Juventus and the New York Cosmos in the US, as well as at Palmeiras back in Brazil. Chinesinho had put down roots in the Veneto region and was keen to return to his adopted country. Bassano was a tiny club, but it gave him the opportunity to manage and, most of all, stay involved in football.

One day, the club president, Renato Sonda, told him he was concerned about the club's youth academy. He said that the kids wanted to learn, but good youth coaches were difficult to find. Too many coaches working with young kids saw themselves as tactical specialists, looking to win at all costs rather than develop the youngsters, teach them the game and, above all, allow them to have fun while learning. What to do?

'I know,' Chinesinho said, his face lighting up. 'Let me call Djalma. If I ask him, I'm sure he'll come. We're good friends and he's not doing much these days.'

'Djalma?'

'Yeah, Djalma . . . Djalma Santos, I mean!' Sonda's jaw probably dropped to the floor. Djalma Santos was arguably the greatest right-back in the history of the game. He was a fixture on the 1958 and 1962 Brazil sides that won consecutive World Cups: the same team that featured Didi, Bellini, Mário Zagallo and, of course, a guy named Pelé. Santos played in four World Cups and retired with ninety-eight caps, more than anyone in the history of the Brazilian national team. He was, literally, a living legend. And Chinesinho was telling him that he would pick up and move 5,000 miles away to the Italian countryside to teach ten year olds about football?

Really?

Really. A few weeks later, Djalma showed up in Bassano with his wife and daughter. They found him and his family an apartment just outside the centre of town and he got to work with enthusiasm and humility. Before every training session, he'd walk all over the pitch removing stones and divots. He was probably the only groundskeeper in history with two World Cup winner's medals.

His Italian was rudimentary, but his love of children and teaching was unmatched. Or, perhaps, matched only by his love of football. The kids took to him straight away, not least because he taught them to take risks, to try difficult moves, to attempt that back heel or flick with the outside of the boot. That's how you have fun. That's how you grow as a player.

When word got out that *the* Djalma Santos was right there, living in a modest flat in Bassano and teaching football, other local clubs beat a path to Sonda's door. 'You can't have Djalma Santos here among us and not share him! Please let him come and speak to our kids . . . please!' And so, he moonlighted, regularly working with the Bassano Academy, then hopping in the car to visit football schools up and down Veneto. He didn't mind. He was in his element.

He ended up staying in Italy for two years and, to many, it still seems like a fairy tale that he was ever there, among them. Not for glory or money, but just to have a new experience and impart his love of the game.

One of his charges, Massimiliano Sambugaro, now a youth coach himself, shared the following anecdote a few years ago: 'I had scuffed my shot and I angrily blamed the ball, which was old and somewhat threadbare. Djalma turned to me and said: "It's never the fault of the ball, it's always the fault of the guy kicking it. Remember, there is no such thing as a bad football. Every football is beautiful."'

As beautiful as a man with two World Cup trophies at home who travels halfway around the world to a small town to teach kids how to love the game as much as he did.

'IT'S IMPOSSIBLE TO BEAT A PERSON WHO NEVER GIVES UP.'

68

ROGER DE VLAEMINCK

Roger De Vlaeminck liked to say that sometimes the bike carried him and sometimes he carried the bike. But they were always together: a single entity. Before the 1973 Milan–San Remo cycle race, he noticed that his team owner, Giorgio Perfetti, drove a shiny blue Ferrari.

'Win today and I'll buy you one just like it,' Perfetti told him. De Vlaeminck duly won the race and, a few weeks later, the blue Ferrari showed up at his home. Except less than a month later, he returned it. Why?

'This is a footballer's car, not one for a cyclist,' De Vlaeminck said, as the story goes. 'I have to take the whole bike apart to fit it in the boot. It's hugely impractical and a pain.' The cost of running the car might have had something to do with his decision.

That was De Vlaeminck. It didn't occur to him that a Ferrari is about the drive, the hum of the engine, the thrill of the acceleration as well as, yes, the status it confers. Nope. It was about getting from point A to point B. And, sure, it was pretty, but if it couldn't take him and the bike in a way that was convenient and efficient, it wasn't going to work for him. Because he sure as heck wasn't going to leave his bike at home. That would be unthinkable.

De Vlaeminck was a gifted rider who made his name early on in cyclocross – hence his aptitude for carrying the bike – as well as on roads. He was known for his intensity, especially in difficult racing circumstances. The Paris–Roubaix, the classic one-day race over cobblestones, often in muddy, rainy conditions, was very much his speciality, to the point that he won it four times.

But he was also brutally honest and practical. He was a ferocious competitor, whose record in one-day races was unmatched. He is one of only three cyclists to have won all five of the 'Monuments of Cycling': the Milan–San Remo three times, the Paris–Roubaix four times, the Giro di Lombardia twice, and the Tour of Flanders and Liège-Bastogne-Liège once each. In total, he won 255 one-day races of every stripe over his fifteen-year career ('And I could have won many more,' he said).

And yet, when it came to the great stage races like the Tour de France or Giro d'Italia, he often came up short. He gave his reasons for it without any shame, but rather with typical directness: 'I could sustain pressure, tremendous pressure, but only for so long . . . after a day or two, I had to disconnect mentally . . . I simply couldn't handle staying focused and mentally in the race for weeks and weeks.'

De Vlaeminck's introspection led to another realisation. Throughout the mid-1970s, one of his great rivals had been his fellow countryman Freddy Maertens. They were teammates for many years and appeared to loathe each other. It frustrated their team principals no end that they had paid handsomely for two of the best riders in the world, and yet those two riders actively got in each other's way.

At the 1975 road race world championships, for example, Maertens did not help De Vlaeminck, who was the favourite that year. The pair spent so much time competing with each other that De Vlaeminck ended up finishing second. The following year at the Tour of Flanders, the two engaged in a personal battle of sudden attacks early in the race, which to most observers seemed pointless. Neither man won thanks to De Vlaeminck's obsession with Maertens, and vice versa.

And so, De Vlaeminck took matters into his own hands. He called up Maertens directly and laid out the facts. The following is an imagined reconstruction.

'Freddy, it's Roger, we need to end this now. We are hurting each other's careers. Let's strike a deal.'

'Roger, you're right. We're both less successful than we deserve because we spend so much time and energy fighting each other rather than simply winning races. A deal would make sense, but there's a problem . . .'

'What's that?'

'I really don't like you. And, more important than that, I don't trust you. Not at all. I can't make a deal with a person who I don't trust.'

'If that's all it is, I have the perfect solution . . .'

And, with that De Vlaeminck summoned a lawyer and had a formal agreement put together. They laid out conditions and decided not to compete with each other, except in certain circumstances. It came right down to the race calendar. One would have the support of the other in certain races and vice versa. It was all notarised and official.

And, sure enough, the following year, at the 1977 Tour of Flanders, De Vlaeminck and Maertens found themselves alone at the head of the race. Maertens was true to his word. He cycled behind De Vlaeminck for the final kilometres, making no attempt to challenge him. That day was De Vlaeminck's day. Maertens would have his shot in the next race.

'LIFE IS NOT WAITING FOR THE STORM TO PASS. IT'S ABOUT LEARNING TO DANCE IN THE RAIN.'

69

MAGIC JOHNSON

In the autumn of 1991, Earvin 'Magic' Johnson had the world at his feet. He was regarded by many as the greatest point guard in the history of the National Basketball Association. He had played twelve years in the league and won five championships and three Most Valuable Player awards.

But there was more to it than that. He was also one of the most popular players in the league, a charismatic figure whose rivalry with Larry Bird of the Boston Celtics had regenerated the NBA, attracting new generations of fans worldwide and jumpstarting a league that had looked moribund fifteen years earlier. It's not a coincidence that the two of them, together with Michael Jordan, who arrived a few seasons later, were credited with laying the foundation of the sporting juggernaut it is today.

Johnson's team, the Los Angeles Lakers, were one of those rare dominant sides that weren't hated by neutrals, and that had a lot to do with Magic. He was selfless on the court, and not just because of the position he played, dishing out assists to others, but also because of the sacrifices he made. At six feet, nine inches tall, he was an atypical point guard, a big man with the ball skills of a smaller man, and he had readily played other positions, including centre (where he lined up against seven-footers) to help the team. He and his wife, Cookie, were expecting a child. He had plenty of interests beyond basketball, and sponsors loved his charisma and the articulate way in which he spoke. Some saw a future for him in politics or showbusiness. And then there was that smile: the 'Magic' smile, the one to which it was impossible to say no.

And then came 7 November 1991, and a press conference in Los Angeles where he told the world that he had contracted HIV, the virus that causes AIDS, and would be retiring from basketball, effective immediately.

For many, it was a 'Where were you when you heard?' moment, not unlike the Kennedy assassination. It was a body blow. AIDS had been in the mainstream consciousness for less than a decade. It was still seen as 'the gay disease' at a time when many people were openly homophobic.

Magic would later reveal that he had contracted the illness after living a promiscuous lifestyle. He wasn't gay, but he had slept with dozens of women, mostly on the road. In the twisted ethos of the time, he drew fire from all sides. Many spread rumours that he was secretly gay and simply incapable of owning up to it. Others chastised him for his infidelity and for the pain he was putting his young wife and unborn son through: not just the HIV, but the scrutiny.

Magic faced it all, with honesty and transparency. What's more, he continued to speak out about how he contracted HIV: through unprotected heterosexual sex. The idea that straight men could be at risk of contracting HIV or AIDS by having unprotected sex with women simply hadn't entered the mainstream consciousness: it was something doctors and teachers told young men, but not something they believed or took precautions against.

Magic changed all that. A few months after his announcement, despite his official retirement, fans voted him into the NBA All-Star game. Despite some players feeling he shouldn't play, fearing the risk of contamination, Magic not only played, but was named MVP of the game.

The day turned into a celebration of Magic and his courage and openness.

That summer he was chosen for the 'Dream Team': for the first time in Olympics history, NBA stars were allowed to play in the Games, and the 1992 Olympic team is thought to be the greatest ever assembled. Magic won his gold medal amidst standing ovations. People began to see that HIV-positive people could live with the virus. It was not an instant death sentence.

A few years later, he even returned as a player. His comeback only lasted one season – he was thirty-seven at the time – but his return was a result of the intense physical work he put in, not just to be fit enough to play basketball, but to stave off the effects of HIV.

Nearly three decades after his announcement, Magic continues to work as an entrepreneur, commentator and HIV activist. After his diagnosis, he could have chosen a quiet retirement, away from the limelight and the pressures and responsibility. Instead, he chose to educate and continue his work around the world.

His basketball skill and his smile charmed us. But it was his words and actions after his diagnosis that taught us that AIDS and HIV were issues that affected all of us, and had to be tackled globally.

'AS LONG AS YOU WORRY ABOUT WHAT OTHERS THINK, YOU BELONG TO THEM.'

70

MARTINA NAVRATILOVA

The year was 1975. Martina Navratilova was a teenager with a youthful face and a bowl cut of brown hair. But she was already the leader of the Czechoslovakian team that had just won the Federation Cup, beating Ireland, the Netherlands, West Germany, France and Australia, the latter without losing a set to the heavily favoured Evonne Goolagong and Helen Gourlay.

She was a national hero and a budding star. The Czechoslovak government gave her a reward: an exit visa to travel to Boston to compete in a tournament. But it came with a stern warning: 'You'll need to tell us everywhere you go. And if you don't do as we say, your career is over.'

She had been to the US before, competing in various tournaments from the age of sixteen. But that was different. Back then she had been a chaperoned child. Now she was an adult and she'd be travelling on her own. What's more, she had been tempted to defect for some time, although she wasn't sure she could find it in her heart to leave her family: her mother Jana, her stepfather Miroslav and, perhaps most of all, her grandmother, Agnes.

She knew the story of her compatriot Jaroslav Drobny, who had fled Czechoslovakia with his Davis Cup teammate Vladimir Cernik in 1949. Drobny was stateless for a while before acquiring Egyptian citizenship, winning Wimbledon and later becoming a British subject. That had been a long time ago, however. What spooked Navratilova was that she hadn't shared her thoughts on defection with anyone and yet, somehow, the Czechoslovak government seemed to know.

She duly won the Boston tournament and immediately enrolled in another, in Amelia Island, but she declined to notify the government or the Czechoslovak federation. When they found out, the day before the final, she received a telegram ordering her home immediately. She ignored it and, the next day, lost the final against Chris Evert. Only then, after competing, did she fly back to Prague.

The government was unnerved by her behaviour. They noticed just how friendly she had appeared to be with Evert (who, of course, would later become her great rival). Still, they reflected that she was young and, in the end, had not defected but had flown home as instructed. Martina got away with a stern dressing down.

Shortly thereafter she filed for a visa to play at the French Open. This was granted on one condition: she must not fraternise with players from the West, but instead limit her interactions to fellow Eastern Europeans. What did Martina do? Not only did she fraternise with whoever she liked, she connected with Evert and the two paired up to play – and win – the French Open women's doubles. They even shared a hotel room for a while.

This did not sit well with the Czech authorities. They threatened her further, but knew they could only push it so far: after all, she was one of the country's biggest stars. She knew that the US Open later that summer was her best chance to leave once and for all. She resolved to tell her family, but she couldn't bring herself to do it. She was genuinely terrified that they would implore her to stay.

She reached the semi-final of the US Open, where she was due to face – who else? – Evert. The night before the semi-final, she called home and, fighting back tears, told her family that she wouldn't be returning.

'If you're going to stay, then stay,' Miroslav told her. 'But whatever happens, don't come home. And be prepared: know they will probably use us to pressure you and guilt you into returning. If that happens, don't listen to us. Don't come back until things change here.'

The following day, after losing the semi-final, Navratilova travelled from Forest Hills to Manhattan to apply for asylum. She held a press conference in which she was careful to avoid politics: 'I have applied for political asylum in the United States. This is neither an ideological choice nor a political one; it's simply about my career. If I am not free to enter the tournaments I choose to enter, when I choose to enter them, I'll never become the best player in the world.'

The response from Czechoslovakia came two weeks later, via the Czech Tennis Federation. 'Martina Navratilova has shown scorn for the proletariat. Czechoslovakism has given her all the tools and resources for her development but she opted for a professional career and to look after her bank account.'

Propaganda aside, her first months away from home were extremely tough. Martina turned to junk food and gained weight. She was often depressed. But, three months after her request was filed, she was granted asylum and a Green Card. And she embarked on a long and successful tennis career that would see her win eight Wimbledon titles, four US Opens, three Australian Opens and two French Opens.

Along the way, she became one of the first leading athletes to identify in public as first bisexual and then lesbian, later becoming an activist in fields as diverse as gay and lesbian rights, animal rights and body image.

But there was one thing missing: home. Her family and the country of her birth remained in her heart. And so, in 1986, when Czechoslovakia were drawn to face the United States in Prague in the Federation Cup, she faced a dilemma. Could she bear to go home, face the crowd and deal with her past?

The fact that Evert was by her side, supporting her, made all the difference. Her eyes glistened as she listened to the two anthems. And then, when she scored her first point, the Prague crowd regaled her with a standing ovation. Their child prodigy was back home. And there's no place like home.

'YOU ARE SUCCESSFUL IN YOUR FIELD WHEN YOU DON'T KNOW WHETHER YOU ARE WORKING OR PLAYING.'

71

JAMES HUNT

James Hunt was the archetypal racing driver: he was handsome, a playboy off the track and an uber-talented daredevil on it. He made a name for himself not just for his breakneck exploits at the wheel, but also for his fearlessness – some would say recklessness – which often led to crashes, hence his nickname 'Hunt the Shunt'.

Needless to say, he had a rebellious, hyperactive streak from childhood and a charisma that made it nearly impossible for people to turn him down. Men wanted to be him, women wanted to be with him – and sponsors wanted to give him cash. He celebrated his eighteenth birthday at Silverstone and left little doubt as to what he wanted to be when he grew up: a Formula One World Champion.

Auto-racing, of course, is an expensive pursuit, and it's all the more expensive when you're crashing and destroying cars regularly. But he would unfailingly find a way to charm local sponsors into backing his team and he struck gold in the form of an eccentric millionaire in love with the sport: Alexander Hesketh.

Hesketh founded his own team and entered Formula One in 1973, with Hunt at the wheel. They weren't taken particularly seriously. In fact, the joke was that they excelled not at being the fastest but at consuming the most cases of champagne. But Hesketh could also count on a brilliant engineer, Harvey Postlethwaite, to go with his brilliant young driver, and they started winning Grands Prix.

After three years however, Hesketh ran out of money and Hunt was left without a team. He approached McLaren, who were about to sign the experienced Jacky Ickx.

Hunt told them he was faster than Ickx, brimming with his usual confidence.

The McLaren officials replied that they thought Ickx was more experienced, reliable and mature.

Hunt responded by asking if they were looking for a driver or a door-to-door salesman.

Hunt proved that he was indeed fast – very fast. He was also a party animal, perhaps too much so. Plenty of booze and beautiful women flowed through his life, often at the track as well as away from it. The consensus was that McLaren had made a mistake. Becoming Formula One World Champion was, above all, about discipline.

Except Hunt would prove them wrong. He won the 1976 title by winning the final race in a veritable rainstorm in Japan, going all out with a visibility of no more than thirty metres.

Having achieved his goal – to become world champion – everything seemed anticlimactic. He raced for a few more years, without much enthusiasm, devoting most of his energy to women and partying. After all, once you've won, doing it again isn't quite as much fun, is it? At least not in his mind.

The passion that drove him to excel on the track ebbed away. The one that pushed him to his limits in the bedroom and at the bar remained.

'SOMETIMES DECIDING WHO YOU ARE IS DECIDING WHO YOU'LL NEVER BE AGAIN.'

72

CAITLYN JENNER

For most of her life, she was known for two things. First, as a world-class athlete and Olympic gold medallist, the very picture of American wholesomeness, whose image adorned an iconic box of cereal. Second, as a hen-pecked reality television parent, whose fly-on-the-wall series spawned plenty of imitators and spin-offs.

Bruce Jenner, as Caitlyn was known until 2015, was hugely comfortable with fame and celebrity. Jenner was a star from early childhood, eventually going to the 1976 Olympics in Montreal and capturing gold in the Decathlon, shattering the world record along the way. The cameras loved Jenner's All-American good looks and Jenner loved the camera back, distributing the right poses, whether draped in the American flag post-race (something commonplace today, but unprecedented at the time) or stopping to smile and flex.

Jenner was considered to play Superman on the big screen (the role eventually went to Christopher Reeve). Jenner posed nude for *Playgirl*. Jenner appeared regularly playing a motorcycle cop on the show *CHiPs*. Jenner's name was put on everything, from gyms to aviation companies. And, of course, there were the Wheaties, for whom Jenner became a de facto spokesperson. Jenner was everyone's knight in shining armour, at once aspirational and unattainable.

And then, as Jenner got older, there was a shift. No longer Superman, but Everyman, or more specifically, Celebrity Everyman. Jenner appeared on countless shows, from *I'm a Celebrity . . . Get Me Out of Here!* to *The Apprentice*, as well as making numerous cameos as – who else? – Bruce Jenner. This new celebrity Jenner, still wholesome, was a parent, able to be self-deprecating and even goofy.

Jenner's third marriage had been to Kris Kardashian, herself a minor celebrity. Each of them had four children from previous relationships, and they went on to have two of their own, Kendall and Kylie, bringing the total to ten. What followed, in 2007, was one of the most impactful – and discussed – reality series of all time, *Keeping Up with the Kardashians*. Jenner wasn't the focus – the kids, Kim, Khloe, Kourtney, Kylie and Kendall, stole the show – but Jenner was always there, like a sitcom parent.

And then came the moment in which Bruce left and the world met Caitlyn. She appeared in public for the first time in the course of a television interview. Caitlyn told the world that she had dealt with gender dysphoria ever since she was a child. It's a condition in which a person experiences a mismatch between their gender identity and the sex assigned them at birth. In Caitlyn's case it must have been all the more strident, because Bruce was a sort of idealised hyper-masculine superman, literally the greatest athlete in the world.

In a follow-up interview, she revealed that she had kept her true identity hidden from all but very few close friends and that now, for the first time, she felt free. Free to be herself. Free to express who she was.

Some were cynical, noting the public nature of her announcement and the media appearances that followed, including an eight-part documentary and a special episode of *Keeping Up with the Kardashians*, which chronicled her family's questions and reactions. But, in fact, considering how Jenner had always lived life – in a perpetual goldfish bowl of media scrutiny, most of it invited in – it should not be surprising that Caitlyn's entrance into the world was equally stage-managed and in the public eye.

This is who she was, both when she appeared as Bruce and now that she was Caitlyn. But that should not minimise the courage it took for Caitlyn to take that step. She knew the world loved and embraced Bruce the Olympian, Bruce the Pitchman, Bruce the professional celebrity and Bruce the hen-pecked, goofy dad in a mad, showbiz family. But she genuinely had no idea how the world would react to Caitlyn, whether Caitlyn would be shunned, starved of the daily celebrity that Jenner had enjoyed so much.

She got her answer. While there was some controversy, most admired the courage behind her leap into the unknown. And, more importantly, she instantly became the most famous trans woman in the world. She brought attention to the issue of gender dysphoria like never before. And she sent a message to so many people – whether gay or straight, cis or trans – about the importance of being themselves. She, rightly and proudly, can add a third thing to her list of reasons why Caitlyn Jenner is famous.

'WORK UNTIL YOUR IDOLS BECOME YOUR RIVALS.'

73

LEON SPINHS

On 25 February 1964, virtually all of America stopped and gathered around the television. Sonny Liston, the fierce, tough-as-nails, ex-convict heavyweight champion of the world, was facing Cassius Clay (who would soon after become Muhammad Ali) in Miami, Florida. The latter was a former Olympic gold medallist and a media darling, but also an eight-to-one underdog.

Watching more than 1,000 miles away in Saint Louis, Missouri, was an eleven-year-old boy named Leon Spinks. Young Leon lived in what you might call the rough part of town, raised by his mother and rarely seeing his father. All around him were poverty, crime and broken homes. But for the duration of that fight, he was transported elsewhere, to a world where men became titans, fighting mano-a-mano with the world watching.

Leon wanted to box, but he knew opportunities were few and far between where he was from. What practice he could get often consisted of getting into fights. Or, as he would later put it in an interview in the *Guardian*: 'If you couldn't box, you'd get your ass whipped. We took a lot of ass-whipping when we started.'

He joined the United States Marine Corps while still in his teens to get away from the drugs and crime in his neighbourhood, but also in the hope that it would provide him with a pathway to the boxing ring. Sure enough, while in the military he was given his chance. He won three US amateur boxing titles in the light heavyweight category and went on to box for the United States at the 1976 Olympics in Montreal. Throughout, he continued to follow Ali's career, drawing inspiration as he tracked his ups and downs through world titles and iconic fights, political outspokenness, and the three-year exile in his prime for his opposition to the Vietnam War.

Leon returned from the Olympics with the gold medal and turned professional soon after, making his debut in January 1977. Some six months later, his promoter got a call from Muhammad Ali's people. The world heavyweight champion was going to have to defend his title against Ken Norton the following year. It would be the fourth time Ali had faced Norton and he needed a warm-up bout before that, just something to keep him on his toes ahead of a clash with an opponent who knew him very well. He would consider Leon as an opponent, if he could beat an Italian fighter, Alfio Righetti.

Sure enough, that November, Leon took to the ring against Righetti, beating him by going the distance over ten rounds. It was a tough bout. In old footage of the fight, when the decision is announced, Leon can be seen celebrating as if he were a child. In many ways, that's understandable. He was just a young boxer, with seven professional fights under his belt, and he'd now have a shot at taking on his idol, the man who had turned him on to boxing thirteen years earlier.

The Ali of the late 1970s, while still heavyweight champion, wasn't the all-conquering force of his early career. By the time the fight rolled around, he was thirty-six years old, and, in his recent outings, had looked a little less agile and a little more laboured than the whirlwind who would, as he himself put it, 'float like a butterfly and sting like a bee'. But he was still the undisputed number one, with a record of fifty-five wins and just two defeats.

The media expected Ali to squash Leon, and had already started preparing for the fourth Ali–Norton bout. Leon was a ten-to-one underdog, but he was determined not to simply be an appetiser for Ali to whet his appetite before his 'real' title defence. Leon trained maniacally, for as many as ten hours a day, and was single-minded in his pursuit. He knew that very few people get the opportunity to face their heroes and he was not going to squander it.

The fight began with a furious Leon dominating Ali for the best part of four rounds. It was as if the champion was stunned, unprepared for the hell his young challenger was unleashing. But then Ali found his footing and Leon began to tire. And from round five to round nine, it was obvious who the champ was. Ali was surgical in his dismantling of Leon, even pulling out the old swagger.

Most observers felt Ali would end the fight in the tenth round. After all, Leon had never gone beyond ten rounds and his knees were already wobbly. And sure enough, Ali began to deliver his onslaught, only for Spinks to not just resist, but to seemingly grow in strength. Whatever energy he had lost in the middle of the fight was returning. When the fight ended, after twelve rounds, with both men still on their feet, most were incredulous. Leon celebrated, pumping his fist and jumping into the embrace of his corner men. He had already won just by making it here and going this distance.

But there was more. Had this brash young man, who was supposed be a patsy for Ali, really subverted the established order? The judge's verdict was split but fell in Leon's favour. Leon jumped around the ring, both hands in the air. Dreams did come true.

The circle was complete. Just as a young Olympic gold medallist had upset the champion Liston fourteen years earlier, now that very same prize fighter found himself upset by another young Olympic gold medallist. Just as then, it was a stunning upset that nobody had anticipated.

'WHEN A FLOWER DOESN'T GROW YOU FIX THE ENVIRONMENT IN WHICH IT GROWS NOT THE FLOWER.'

Alexander Den Heijer

74

GHADA SHOUAA

Ghada Shouaa always stood out. Sport and girls didn't always mix readily growing up in Mahardah, Syria. But her height – she would eventually grow to six foot, three inches – and athleticism were prized. Because while age-old gender stereotypes existed when she reached her teens in the late 1980s (and still exist today in much of the Arab world), her part of the country also valued success. And the tall girl with the quick smile and the strong limbs pretty much excelled at everything she did.

She played handball and basketball, earning a call up to the national youth side in the latter. But, as she would later reveal, she soon realised that she would never achieve world class status on the hardwood court. It's a team game, and this was Syria. No matter how hard she worked, she'd always be playing with and against a very limited pool of players. She knew girls of her age in other parts of the world were travelling across borders, competing against the very best and doing it at a higher level. Without wishing to disrespect her teammates, they were not on her level and would never be.

And so, at sixteen, relatively late in an athlete's life, she chose to pick up an individual sport. Here, she concluded, it would all be down to her and how far she could push her body. Her training wouldn't be that different, in relative

302

terms, to that of the best athletes her age in wealthier, more advanced parts of the world.

The local athletics club knew she would excel at most disciplines. The question was finding the right one for her to really fulfil her potential. She could run, she could throw, she could jump . . . getting her to specialise seemed almost reductive. So, why not do it all? Why not compete in the heptathlon?

This was easier said than done. In Syria at the time, athletics facilities were in high demand, and were used almost exclusively by men. And not every facility catered for every discipline. Some had a track, but no javelin facilities. Others might have a long jump pit, but no circle for the shot put. And even when they did, scheduling training time was difficult. Shouaa dutifully arranged to be driven all over western Syria, cobbling together a schedule that would enable her to train across all seven events. That in itself was tough, before you even got to the extra hurdles of being a woman in a sport dominated by men and being a devout Christian in a nation that was still heavily Muslim.

But when you're determined, there's no stopping you. Ghada gave up much of her social life. All she really did was study and train, train and study. That, and travel interminably between venues. She qualified for the 1991 World Athletics Championships in Tokyo and, in the same year, placed second at the Asian Games. She made it to the Barcelona Olympics in 1992 and finished twenty-fifth, while carrying an injury. Over the next two years, she won gold at the Asian Games.

Suddenly, people began to take notice. Suddenly, life became a little easier. Hafez al-Assad, the Syrian President at the time, sniffed out a PR opportunity and gifted her a house and a Peugeot. She was just grateful that she could now drive herself around the country rather than having to rely on others. After she suffered another injury, al-Assad paid for her rehabilitation in Germany.

She responded by winning gold at the 1995 World Championships and repeated the feat a year later at the Atlanta Olympics, becoming the first Syrian gold medallist in history. So single-minded was her determination that she had no problem working with a coach, Latvian Paris Votes, with whom she could not communicate: Votes spoke no Arabic, she spoke neither Latvian nor Russian. Instead, they relied on an interpreter or, during competition, flashcards. It didn't matter. They were on the same wavelength.

But here's the twist. At every opportunity, even after her retirement, Shouaa has gone out of her way to tell everyone how fortunate she has been. Not because of her God-given ability, not because of her determination, but simply because she was given a chance: something that far too many girls in Syria are denied. And, obviously, with the war, things have only got worse.

'First, you're nobody and nobody knows you,' she says. 'Then you get a break and you become famous. And suddenly you belong to everyone. With that comes responsibility. The responsibility to recognise how you got here and that not everybody is as fortunate as you . . . you have to fight for those who have no opportunity.'

'THERE IS ONLY ONE WAY
TO AVOID CRITICISM:
DO NOTHING, SAY NOTHING
AND BE NOTHING.'

75

ERIC MOUSSAMBANI

At one point, Eric Moussambani is alone. Technically, that's not true. There are thousands watching him in the stands, just a few feet away and tens of millions more watching around the world. But there is nobody with him in the pool. And everybody else is so remote, not just physically but psychologically and empathetically too, that they might as well be in another dimension.

Because frankly, they're not sure of what they're actually seeing. Heck, he's not entirely sure either. He's competing in a qualifying heat for the men's 100-metre freestyle at the 2000 Sydney Olympics. And, as long as he finishes the race, he will win his heat, because the other swimmers – Niger's Karim Bare and Tajikistan's Farkhod Oripov – were disqualified for two false starts each.

Until recently, Eric did not even know how to swim. He has literally never been in a pool this big, the standard, 50-metre Olympic-sized pool. And he is about to become a media sensation.

He struggles, admitting later that the tail end of the second lap was exceptionally difficult, the temptation to just coast very strong. But he wanted to finish and to go as hard as he could. And it really didn't matter that doing his best – one minute, fifty-two seconds – wasn't particularly good by Olympic standards. The gold medallist in the Sydney Games would be more than twice as fast, completing the

100 metres in under forty-nine seconds. And, of course, while winning your heat is nice, it does not guarantee you a place in the next round: it's all down to time. And with his time, which is some fifty seconds slower than the next worst swimmer, it's evident his Olympics are ending there and then, as soon as he gets out of the pool.

But while it may be a cliché, for him it was just about being there, in the truest sense of the Olympic spirit. Equatorial Guinea benefited from a wild card programme of qualifying that gave countries with limited infrastructure or experience in a particular discipline a shot at the Olympic Games, even when athletes didn't meet qualifying standards.

Eric may have been given a wild card, but he sweated and sacrificed just like the guys setting records. For a start, there was no swimming federation in Equatorial Guinea and, therefore, no swimming clubs. No swimming clubs means no public swimming pools, let alone Olympic-sized ones. The best he could muster, with the aid of an old friend, was the opportunity to train in a hotel pool that was thirteen metres long. So as not to disturb the guests, his training time was at five o'clock in the morning, three days a week, and he had to be out of the water an hour later.

So, he found other ways to train. He swam in the sea, he swam in rivers, he worked out in the gym. He picked up basic techniques from fishermen who, after unloading their cargo, showed him how to move his legs, how to stay buoyant. Once in Sydney, he learned how to dive, simply by watching others train. Some of his fellow competitive swimmers asked him what he was doing there, whether he was really going to race. Others offered tips. The South African coach took him under his wing and showed him the basics.

Come race day, however, Eric was once again on his own. Just him and the water and a simple task. Finish the race and show everyone that Equatorial Guinea also belongs to the world of competitive swimming. And if, along the way, he proved what desire, ingenuity and a whole load of hard graft could do for an ordinary man with an extraordinary heart, well, that was a bonus.

'PAIN MAKES YOU STRONGER.'

76

KERRI STRUG

Recent studies have found that sometimes pain is, in fact, an illusion. Sometimes it's not linked to any kind of injury or illness. And sometimes it's merely a warning sign. If you're strong enough, you can will it away.

Standing one metre and forty-one centimetres tall (more like short), Kerri Strug might not strike you as the epitome of strength. But what she did at the 1996 Olympics in Atlanta was nothing short of herculean: forcing her mind to ignore the messages coming from her screaming nerve endings. Put differently, it's not the size of the dog in the fight, it's the size of the fight in the dog. And this little dog had plenty of fight.

The United States were neck-and-neck with Russia in the latter stages of the women's team gymnastics event at Atlanta. They had a commanding lead going into the final round and it would have taken a monumental collapse for the Russians to come back. The Americans did not need high scores, they didn't need to do anything fancy or special or take any risks. They simply needed to complete their vaults without falling or messing up the landing.

But every one of the American women who vaulted in that final rotation somehow scored less than expected, usually by making mistakes in the landing, with an extra step or hop for balance, and, in the case of Dominique Moceanu, falling not once, but twice.

Meanwhile, the Russians, who were on a floor exercise rotation, were racking up excellent scores. The US lead was diminishing with every vault. It came down to the final American gymnast, Strug. On the sidelines, you could see the mood of the US coach, the legendary Béla Károlyi, darken.

At eighteen, Strug was one of the older gymnasts on the team. She wasn't a star: she was there for her experience and work ethic, and the example she set for her younger teammates. She was a fighter, who over the previous four years had struggled with weight issues, illness and injury, determined to make it to the Olympic squad. That said, the odd thing about Strug was she tended to perform far better in practice than in competition. The coach's fear was that the pressure of the moment, the performance anxiety of knowing that a gold medal hinged on her vault, would get to her. Not everybody has the mentality of a champion.

Still, what she needed to do was relatively simple at this level: a vault she had successfully performed thousands of times (maybe tens of thousands, given how maniacal Károlyi was about training and repetition), except Strug too couldn't stick the landing, falling backwards and hitting the mat hard. The inevitable low score that would ensue wasn't the worst of it. She felt a sharp pain in her ankle and, as she would later recall, heard an audible snap. She had badly damaged her tendon and suffered a third-degree lateral sprain.

The heavily partisan crowd gasped. Strug looked up in disbelief, propped up on her knees. As she hobbled back to Károlyi wide-eyed, the pain shot up her leg, so intense it made her head throb. All she wanted to know was whether her score would be enough to mathematically secure the gold.

The word came back. If she vaulted again and stuck her landing, gold was guaranteed. If she was unable to go again, the gold was up for grabs: a sterling performance from the Russians in their final floor exercise would see them win it all.

Károlyi walked over to where she was sitting on the floor, icepack on her ankle, tears streaming down her face. He put his arm around her and said: 'Kerri, we need you one more time. One more time for the gold.'

He helped her over to the runway, and she softly recited a prayer. The pain was so strong she had trouble standing, even on one leg. She'd need both to sprint down the runway and get the necessary velocity to execute her vault.

A deep breath, one last look at Károlyi, and she was gone, her mind not so much pushing the pain away as using it as a stimulant, as a hit of pure adrenaline to drive her forward. Up and over she went, sticking the landing perfectly, on both feet. She heard another snap like the one before and quickly folded her injured ankle behind her, all the while keeping her balance. It happened lightning-fast, before she struck the post-jump pose the judges were looking for. One more hop to face the other side and it was over. Her face was a strange medley of pain and elation, bearing a massive smile, the kind gymnasts are taught to put on for the benefit of judges.

And then she collapsed to the mat, sobbing, holding her badly damaged ankle. Károlyi picked her up. He would later carry her to the podium to accept her gold medal. She had put her body on the line for her teammates. But, most of all, she had conquered pain, if only for the time it takes to complete a vault. And that made all the difference.

'YOU ARE A PRODUCT OF YOUR THOUGHTS.'

77

TOM WATSON

Age is just a number. That may be one of those lines that's used to sell us products and make us feel good about ourselves as we get older. Medically, we know it's not true. As we become adults and get older, our bodies start to change and deteriorate. We are not what we were at our peak. We are, biologically speaking, different people.

Yet there's power in that phrase. Tremendous power. The power not to reverse aging – you can't – but to lessen its grip on our minds. And that's the power Tom Watson harnessed in 2009 at the Open Championship in Turnberry, Scotland.

Watson turned professional in 1971, when he was twenty-two. By the middle of the decade, he had established himself as one of the world's best golfers. He was named PGA Player of the Year six times – four of them consecutive between 1977 and 1980 – a number surpassed only by Tiger Woods. Between 1975 and 1984, he won the Masters twice, the Open five times, the US Open once and finished second in the PGA Championship. In five of those years, he was also the top earner on the PGA Tour.

And then . . . he sort of fell away. After 1984, he won one more PGA tournament in the 1980s and two in the 1990s. It was a stark decline that began at the relatively young age (by golf standards) of thirty-five. Watson was one of the more all-round golfers out there and, while he came close on several occasions (he had a share of the lead going into the final round of the 1991 Masters, only to double bogey on the sixth hole and finish third), it was never quite the same.

He hinted at what the problem might be in 1994, at the Open, when he said: 'Sometimes you lose your desire through the years. Any golfer goes through that. When you play golf for a living, like anything in your life, you are never going to be constantly at the top.'

To many it seemed that way. He was a guy who had lost his edge. Still gifted enough to regularly finish among the world's top thirty, but never quite able to regain the magic that had made him the best. If it bothered Watson, he didn't let on. He didn't join the Senior tour, he just kept plugging away. Maybe it was a question of the over-whelming desire leaving him, but him still enjoying golf and competition. Or maybe there were simply many more talented golfers around.

Then came 2009 and the Open at Turnberry. Nobody expected anything from Watson, not least because, by this point, he was fifty-nine years old. Talk of him regaining his mojo had come and gone more than two decades ago. He was what he was: a once-great older golfer who was simply along for the ride.

But then something unexpected happened. Watson rolled through the first round, shooting an astonishing five under par. This put him in second place behind Miguel Ángel Jiménez. After shooting par in the second round, Watson was tied for first place, becoming by some distance the oldest player to have a lead after any round of a major.

He was more than a decade older than Julius Boros, who had won the PGA Championship back in 1968. Was Watson really going to make history and shatter a record many felt might stand forever?

He knew the course at Turnberry well and, of course, had already won the Open there, thirty-two years earlier.

Conditions went from calm and sunny on the first day to windy and showery. In some ways, that suited him. His all-around game was such that he could cope with different conditions. Still, it seemed absurd to think that anyone could win a golf major at fifty-nine, let alone a guy like Watson, eleven years removed from his last tour victory.

But on the third day he came in at one over par and went into the final round with a one-shot lead over Ross Fisher and Matthew Goggin, a two-shot lead over Retief Goosen and Lee Westwood and a three-shot edge over Jim Furyk and Stewart Cink. Watson didn't start well, with two bogeys on his first three holes, and slipped out of the lead. But he regained it with a birdie on the seventeenth hole. And on the very last hole, needing a straightforward par to win, he missed two putts, which left him in a four-hole play-off with Cink.

Were this a Hollywood film, it would have a Hollywood ending. It's not, and it doesn't. It was Cink who came out on top. Twenty years earlier, talk might have been of Watson choking under pressure and bottling it at the last hurdle. Nobody dared say that on this occasion. He had confounded Father Time. And shown over four days, against the world's best golfers, that fifty-nine really was just a number.

'BLOOD, SWEAT, RESPECT:
THE FIRST TWO YOU GIVE,
THE LAST YOU EARN.'

78

PAT TILLMAN

On the surface, Pat Tillman had it all. He had graduated *summa cum laude* ('with highest praise') from university and started a career in the National Football League. Despite being named the Defensive Player of the Year in the Pacific-10 Conference while in college, NFL scouts were a bit sceptical over his size. He was five feet eleven inches: average in real life, but on the small side by NFL standards.

Yet he established himself as a starter for the Arizona Cardinals in his rookie season, 1998, and showed that he had all the tools required by an NFL player. It was during his fourth season, in the aftermath of the 11 September attack on the World Trade Center, that he began to re-evaluate things.

He loved football. Not just the game, but the camaraderie, the fans, the weekly gladiatorial battle. His contract was expiring at the end of the season and the Cardinals, fearing they would lose him as a free agent, offered him $3.6 million over three years. Another team, according to reports, went even higher, putting $9m over five years on the table.

But Tillman chose a different path. On 31 May 2002, along with his brother, Kevin, Tillman enlisted in the military. After basic training, they entered the Rangers, the toughest and most physically and mentally demanding unit in the US Army. The 75th Ranger Regiment, as it is known, specialises in special light infantry operations, often completing the most difficult missions in hostile areas around the world. Less than half those who enlist for Ranger training actually make it through.

Tillman's decision made headlines. Some depicted it as a choice borne purely out of patriotism, or a desire for revenge after the 9/11 attacks due to a deep and profound love for his country. He was instantly celebrated as a hero and a patriot.

Those who knew him well painted a more complex picture. Part of it was Tillman's sense of justice. Here he was, literally playing a game and about to be paid millions for doing so, while other men his own age were going off to war. He had uncles and grandparents who had fought wars and it didn't seem fair that he'd be spared just because of his ability to play sports and play them very well. And there was another element, too. A desire to live life: a desire for adventure, for experience, for making a difference.

For Tillman wasn't the unquestioning flag-waving meathead you might be imagining as you read this. His impressive academic achievements weren't a coincidence. He was an avid reader on all subjects, from politics to religion, and was as comfortable reading Marx as he was the Quran. He searched not for answers, but for more questions. Perhaps what drove him most was not a fear of not knowing something, but a fear of not knowing which questions to ask. Through a friend, he had even made arrangements to meet Noam Chomsky, the well-known pacifist intellectual.

In fact, the military was uneasy about having him at the front. They loved the idea of an NFL star enlisting but tried to steer him towards recruiting efforts back home, wanting to keep him well away from conflict. Why? Not just because Tillman's fame was a very useful recruiting tool for a volunteer army, but also because they genuinely thought he might be a little too inquisitive, a little too clever, a little too much of a free thinker. He was sent for psychological evaluation multiple times, but ultimately was deployed. He wanted to go; they couldn't find a reason to stop him. The fact that he was intelligent and asking questions wasn't enough to keep him at home.

He shipped off first to Iraq and, later, to Afghanistan. He was cynical about the invasion of Iraq and the weapons of mass destruction and felt that, at least in his new deployment, they could make a difference fighting alongside the Afghan army.

He was several years older than most of those he served with and, thanks to his engaging personality, soon became a natural leader. He was known for his generosity and fearlessness. They ultimately cost him his life on 22 April 2004.

He was killed in action after his platoon was ambushed near Sperah in Afghanistan and was immediately hailed as a hero, an example for all young men. The official account stated that his platoon had been effectively split in two after coming under enemy fire. With his platoon mates pinned down a short distance away, Tillman left the relative safety of his own position and charged on foot up a ridge from which the enemy was firing, taking a bullet along the way.

The truth emerged later and it was horrifying. Yes, Tillman died a hero. But he and the Afghan soldier fighting alongside him, both of whom had stormed up that ridge to take on the Al Qaeda fighters, weren't killed by enemy soldiers. It was Tillman's own platoon mates who had shot him, whether because they mistook him for the enemy or because they simply panicked. The account of that day makes for a chilling read, with Tillman on three occasions waving his arms and shouting 'Cease fire! Friendly! Friendly!'.

His body armour and uniform were burned in an apparent attempt to disguise the fact that his death was caused by friendly fire. So too were his notebooks, where he had recorded his personal thoughts on Afghanistan and the war. A congressional inquiry found no evidence of enemy fire on the scene, and established that Tillman had been shot from less than three metres away.

What looked like a cover-up only exacerbated the tragedy. But Tillman's life – and death – remind us that things are often more complex than they appear. While his death was senseless and tragic, if he was driven by a yearning for meaning in life, then his story and sacrifice helped educate many as to the folly of war.

'WE DON'T GROW
WHEN THINGS ARE EASY,
WE GROW WHEN WE
FACE CHALLENGES.'

79

NANCY LIEBERMAN

Looks can be deceiving. And anyone who saw a twelve-year-old Nancy Lieberman would probably never guess what she'd end up doing as a grown-up. She describes her young self as 'just a poor, skinny, redheaded Jewish girl from Queens'. All of this was true – after her parents divorced, she rarely saw her father and, sometimes, there was neither heat nor electricity in her home in Far Rockaway, on the outer edge of New York City – but somewhat reductive.

She was a fiery, wild-haired tomboy who loved sports, especially basketball. Above all, she loved to compete. And that often meant walking up to the local playground in Queens and taking on whoever was there: almost always boys, usually older. Competing against bigger, stronger boys wasn't easy, not least because nobody wanted to play with a girl. And so, Nancy focused on perfecting the one skill she knew would make her an invaluable teammate to every basketball player: being someone who can get them the ball.

She worked extremely hard on passing and ball-handling, secure in the knowledge that it would get her into games. And it did. She'd practice dribbling incessantly and, when it was cold outside, she took it indoors, much to her mother's frustration. Lieberman tells the story of how, annoyed by the noise coming from her room, her mother burst in and punctured the basketball with a screwdriver.

When she found another one and began dribbling again, her mother ruined that one, too. It continued until all five basketballs were flat and Lieberman had no choice but to go outside to find a ball.

Her formative years were all spent on the playground and, indeed, there was something very 'street' to her game. It wasn't just her toughness, it was her intensity, too. She didn't actually play against other girls until she was fifteen.

Once she did, it was obvious that she was a special talent. She was a star in college, twice being named player of the year and, perhaps as important, earning the nickname 'Lady Magic' in honour of Earvin 'Magic' Johnson. Along the way, she played for the United States at the 1976 Olympics in Montreal, winning the silver medal.

With no high-end women's professional league in which to play, she spent much of the next fifteen years bouncing around, finding exhibition games in which to play, turning out for a men's minor league team (the Springfield Fame, where she became the first woman to play in a professional men's competition) and playing for the Washington Generals, the touring opponents of the legendary Harlem Globetrotters.

When the NBA launched a women's league, Lieberman was already thirty-nine years old and hadn't played organised basketball for some fifteen years, but she still managed to stick around for a season. Accepting that her playing career was over, she became determined to coach. She travelled the country attending seminars and courses at her own expense. Her determination was no different than that she had displayed as a little girl on the tarmac playgrounds of Far Rockaway.

She landed a job in the NBDL, the NBA's developmental league, becoming the first woman to coach a men's professional league. A few years later, she was hired as an assistant coach by the Sacramento Kings in the NBA. She held the job for a few seasons until stepping down, aged sixty, to look after her ailing mother.

You'd imagine she'd be left wondering what might have been. What if women's professional basketball had been around when she was in her prime? What if, instead of being effectively self-taught, she'd had intensive coaching from a young age? But, in fact, Lieberman doesn't dwell on that. She proved to the world that looks are deceiving, that skinny red-haired Jewish girls from Queens can become basketball legends . . . and break gender barriers while doing so. As long as they're as steely-eyed and tough as Nancy Lieberman, that is.

'NO MATTER HOW
YOU FEEL — GET UP,
DRESS UP, SHOW UP AND
NEVER GIVE UP.'

80

CAL RIPHEN JUNIOR

The daily rhythm of baseball is unforgiving. No other sport plays as many games: 162 in the regular season. What's more, the campaign runs from early April to early October, which means those 162 games are squeezed into 181 days. And with eighty-one away games, you spend more time on the road than in any other team sport.

Not missing a game all year is difficult. You pick up injuries, you need a rest. Not missing a game for two straight seasons is extremely rare. And if you can manage to play more than three consecutive campaigns without missing a single game, well . . . you're not just special, you're one of only thirty-odd players in the history of baseball to achieve this.

Now consider going more than sixteen years without missing out on a single game. That's what Cal Ripken Junior achieved. His 2,632 consecutive games are more than the total games played of all but thirty-eight men in history. When the streak began on 30 May, 1982, very few people knew what a laptop was. When it ended, people were writing emails on their phones.

It made sense that Ripken would want to play every single game. He grew up immersed in the sport. His father, Cal Senior, was a scout and then manager with the Baltimore Orioles, the only team his son ever played for. Cal Jr was obsessed with the game, hanging out at the

ballpark to glean information from the players and practising obsessively with his brother, Billy, who would also
become a Major Leaguer. He was drafted directly out of
high school by the Orioles in 1978 and made his debut
three years later after some time in the developmental
minor leagues.

The following spring, the streak began. Ripken was
an early success, winning the league MVP award in 1983,
the same year he guided the Orioles to the World Series.
For the next decade, he was a constant in the team, never
quite repeating his batting heroics, but becoming its leader
through his soft-spoken charisma and, well, the fact that he
was always there.

As he entered the 1990s, fans began to speculate about
whether he could break the 56-year-old consecutive game
record of 2,130 games, held by Lou Gehrig. Ripken's prod-
uctivity at bat declined and some questioned whether he
wouldn't benefit from a break. But on he went. The night
he surpassed Gehrig, in September 1995, both the US President Bill Clinton and his Vice President, Al Gore, were in
attendance.

Many expected Ripken to finally take his day off, since
there was no way anybody was going to get close to that
mark. But he persevered, wanting to break the world
record, held by Sachio 'Iron Man' Kinugasa, who had
played 2,215 games in a row in the Japanese league. Ripken
passed him in 1996.

'OK, now he can stop,' many thought. 'There is nobody
left to chase.' But Ripken bristled at this. He was going to
continue for as long as he was selected to start and as long
as his body allowed. It wasn't until the final home game of
the 1998 campaign that he decided to give himself a rest.
He did it by doing something he had never done before in
his life. He approached the manager and asked for a day
off. He wasn't injured, he didn't have anywhere he wanted
to be. He just wanted to be in control of when and where

the feat that dominated his professional life was going to end.

How do you achieve such longevity? Ripken was never suspended and never got into a contractual dispute. Fine, he could control that. He was fortunate that both his children were born during the off-season, so he could be there for their births. He was also lucky that he never suffered any serious debilitating injuries, though on several occasions he played with muscle strains and, for a spell, with nerve damage so bad that he could not sit down in the dugout.

Overall though, he liked to say that it wasn't a big deal. You got ready to play and, if you were ready, you played. He made sure he was ready.

'Normal folks go to work every day, don't they?' Ripken once said. 'What I do is no different.'

'DON'T DOWNGRADE YOUR DREAM JUST TO FIT YOUR REALITY. UPGRADE YOUR CONVICTION TO MATCH YOUR DESTINY.'

81

LEICESTER CITY

Three words that read like the sort of verdict you don't get to appeal.

'Claudio Ranieri? Really?'

That was a tweet from Gary Lineker, favourite son of Leicester City and one of the great forwards in the history of the English game, as well as the host of the BBC's *Match of the Day*. He was referring to the appointment of Ranieri as his old club's new manager.

Ranieri was sixty-four years old and, while he had managed a host of big clubs – from Inter to Juventus, from Chelsea to Monaco, from Roma to Valencia – he had never stayed anywhere very long or won major silverware other than two domestic cups, the most recent of which had been at Valencia nearly two decades earlier. Leicester had narrowly avoided relegation the year before and most supporters wanted a manager who could build a success-ful club over time, not a guy who was, at best, an itinerant short-term solution.

To make matters worse, Esteban Cambiasso, arguably Leicester City's best player the year before, had left via free agency. What were they left with? Like many yo-yo clubs, perennially bouncing up and down between the top two tiers of the English game, they were in a constant state of flux.

When you inhabit the bottom half of the table, the equation is fairly simple. Your good players generally leave you to join bigger clubs who can pay them more, so you either have to figure out how to make it work with your less-gifted players, or hope that you can unearth talent further down the food chain.

Ranieri surveyed his new squad to try and figure out how things would work, and found a colourful, rag-tag bunch. It seemed like everybody had a story. Jamie Vardy was a direct, speedy forward who was still playing amateur football into his early twenties and had a conviction for assault which forced him to play for six months with an electronic ankle tag. Winger Marc Albrighton's mother-in-law had been killed in a terrorist attack just a few months earlier. Their captain, Wes Morgan, also came via the amateur game, after escaping gangland violence as a teenager. The new defensive midfielder, N'Golo Kanté, came from the French second division and looked so small and young that he was mistaken for a child looking to join the youth academy by staff when he first arrived. Perhaps their most skilful player was Riyad Mahrez, a Franco-Algerian who also came from the second tier and who, while gifted, was deemed to not have the heart and courage to make his talent count.

The expectation was for a year-long battle to avoid the drop. Bookmakers gave them a three-to-one chance of getting relegated and a 5,000-to-one chance of winning the title. 5,000-to-one are basically throwaway odds: numbers bookies quote to entice some fool to bet on the virtually impossible.

And yet, by late November, they were at the top of the table. Everybody expected them to fall away and, while they did slip into second for a few weeks around Christmas, they were back in first by January. The experts said the pressure would get to them, but what they failed to understand was that pressure comes from expectation. And Leicester's expectations had already been surpassed . . . they were playing with house money. Or, as Ranieri would later put it, living an impossible dream.

He did his part, of course. He shielded the players as best he could, keeping them grounded by celebrating the fact that they had mathematically avoided relegation when they were in first place. Or by raising an imaginary bell and saying 'dilly-ding, dilly-dong' whenever he felt the players were losing focus or getting ahead of themselves.

They won the title on 2 May 2016, when Tottenham Hotspur failed to win away to Chelsea, meaning that, with two matches to play, nobody could surpass their points total. Most of the players watched the match together at Vardy's house, their celebrations quickly spreading around the world via social media. Ranieri had flown to Italy that day to have lunch with his nonagenarian mother, flying back in time for the game on a plane laid on by the club's owner. He watched the match at home and would later describe it as an out-of-body experience, as if he was watching himself and his wife from on high.

And that's how it felt to many. A dream: a surreal, impossible dream. You don't win a Premier League title as 5,000-to-one underdogs just by being the best you can be. It also takes luck, self-belief and your opponents stumbling at the right time. But most of all, perhaps, it takes the ability to dream, to visualise, to imagine that the unthinkable can be willed into existence. Even if it's only once every 5,000 years . . .

'BE STRONG.
YOU NEVER KNOW
WHO YOU ARE
INSPIRING.'

82

JOE LOUIS

If sport is a social currency that helps bring people together, creates connections and makes them feel part of a greater whole, then that's exactly what Joe Louis did. He wasn't America's first black world heavyweight champion – that would be Jack Johnson – but he was the first African American superstar who was universally adored by black and white alike. He was the Michael Jordan of his age.

Perhaps it took somebody of Louis's background to exorcise, however fleetingly, the shame of slavery and segregation. His great grandfather was a white slave owner, three of his grandparents were black slaves, and another was Cherokee Native American. His mother and his father (who was forcibly institutionalised in a psychiatric hospital when Louis was a small child) were sharecroppers in rural Alabama, until the actions of the Ku Klux Klan drove the family to migrate north, to Detroit. That's a lot of dark history contained in just a couple of generations.

He went to vocational school to learn cabinet-making and in his spare time took violin lessons. A friend introduced him to boxing and that's where he, literally, became Joe Louis. Rather than using his last name, Barrow, he opted for his middle name, unsure of whether his mother would approve of his new interest. By the age of twenty he had turned pro at the urging of his managers, John Roxborough and Julian Black.

In one sense, they were extremely entrepreneurial. They knew they had a special talent on their hands, but they also knew that to really cash in, they had to make him palatable to white America: a white America that was all too often racist towards and prejudiced against boxers of colour. So, Roxborough and Black drew up rules for Louis to follow. Live clean: no drinking, no smoking. Fight clean and fair. Never gloat over an opponent, especially a white man. And never, ever, allow yourself to be photographed with a white woman.

Today, it might seem absurd, bordering on pandering. But Louis trusted Roxborough, who was also black. And his success – not just in the ring, but in the media too – proved that Roxborough was right, at least in that era. As Louis rose meteorically through the heavyweight division – with success including wins over Primo Carnera and Max Baer – white mainstream America embraced him in a way that no other boxer of colour had ever been embraced. He was entertaining, powerful and likeable, without any menace that might have allowed the audience to indulge in whatever racist prejudices they might have held.

His fame and popularity crossed the ocean and when he squared off against the German Max Schmeling in 1936, he was heavily favoured. But by this stage, Louis had taken up golf and become obsessed with the game: so much so that it cut into his training time. On the day of the fight, Schmeling, a consummate, methodical professional who was very well prepared, outlasted Louis over twelve rounds.

Instantly, Schmeling was seized upon by the Nazi propaganda machine. In their minds, he was the Teutonic hero, whose racial superiority and intelligence had seen him defeat the inferior American of African descent.

Louis went on to become world champion, defeating James Braddock and retaining his title in other fights, but Nazi Germany still mocked him. And while America adored him, some still had the nagging sense that he

336

wouldn't really prove himself unless he took on – and beat – Schmeling in a rematch. Louis himself admitted he had unfinished business.

By the time the fight rolled around in 1938, the hype and propaganda machines were in full force. Both sides ratcheted up the pressure and doubled down. Schmeling was accompanied by a Nazi publicist, who reminded everyone of the supposed superiority of the Aryan race. Louis had the weight not just of African Americans on his shoulders, but the whole country: after all, he was America's hero.

Louis and Schmeling faced each other in front of 70,000 fans at Yankee Stadium. The bout, arguably the biggest pre-war sporting event in the world, was broadcast around the world. Louis was a dervish that night and ended up knocking Schmeling down three times before the German's corner, mercifully, threw in the towel. The fight lasted just two minutes and four seconds.

America's hero had triumphed. The Nazis had been repelled. Louis was at once a hero and an inspiration to black America at a time when they were largely invisible (Malcolm X famously said that every African American boy wanted to be him), but he was also so much more. Louis was an icon for all Americans. So much so that Jimmy Cannon, one of America's finest sportswriters, probably put it best: 'Yes, Joe Louis is a credit to his race – the human race.'

'LIFE DOES NOT GET EASIER, YOU JUST GET STRONGER.'

83

ELENA DELLE DONNE

The year was 2008 and Elena Delle Donne was the number one ranked girls' high school basketball player in the United States. The next step was choosing where to go to college and further develop her skills before, inevitably, turning professional. The obvious choice was the University of Connecticut, where legendary coach Geno Auriemma had won five national titles (he now has a record eleven), churning out an impressive list of future Olympians and WNBA stars.

Delle Donne duly committed to join Auriemma's team and travelled up for the pre-season summer school programme. After just two days, however, she walked out and returned home. Why? Family: specifically her older sister, Lizzie.

Lizzie is her big sister and has always been a central figure in Elena's life – despite the fact that Lizzie has never spoken to Elena or even seen her. Lizzie was born deaf and blind, with cerebral palsy and autism. Later, she developed spina bifida as well. But such is the closeness of the Delle Donne family, that Elena quickly realised she could not bear to be apart from her sister, even if meant jeopardising a successful basketball career.

And so, she returned home, enrolling instead at her local college, the University of Delaware, so she could be just a 15-minute drive away from her family. Not only that, she also gave up basketball for a year, opting instead to play volleyball. It meant less travel and more time with Lizzie, but also the opportunity to evaluate her next steps after the trauma of being away from her sister.

Elena reflected on her own challenges. A year earlier, she had contracted Lyme disease, and the condition would later be diagnosed as chronic. That would mean coping with daily fever, pain and fatigue. Even now, she takes a cocktail of pills each day and eats a severely modified diet. Elena's height – she is six feet, five inches tall – while obviously an asset on the basketball court, had also been problematic when she was a little girl. She was already six feet tall by the age of thirteen, and doctors had wanted to put her on medication to stunt her growth.

But whatever difficulties she had to face were nothing compared to the challenges her sister faces each and every day. Lizzie needs constant assistance and watching her struggle with daily tasks that others take for granted fuelled Elena's drive to overcome her own challenges.

'She's the best role model in the world,' Elena says. 'Whenever I think of my struggles, I think about how she can't see the sky or the grass, can't talk or walk unassisted.'

Lizzie communicates with the three senses she has. Touch (she'll feel your hand), smell (she'll come close and smell you) and taste (she might lick your face). And over time, that built as close a relationship as any.

Delle Donne's college career at Delaware was a classic example of an outstanding player on a mediocre team. She dominated and carried her teammates, but clearly it meant playing with and practising against far inferior players than she would have done in Connecticut. Did it affect her development? Probably, although what she has been achieving in the WNBA is nothing short of stellar anyway. She was selected for the All-Star team in six of her seven seasons and twice was named the league's

MVP. And she won gold with the United States at the Rio de Janeiro Olympics in 2016.

It has certainly hurt her financially. Unlike most WNBA players, she doesn't play abroad during the six-month long off-season. Most stars use this as a way to top up their salaries and they often earn more away from the WNBA than they do back home. But that would mean spending months at a time away from Lizzie, which would be unthinkable for her. In the bigger picture, it's a small sacrifice to make for someone who has been so central to your life.

Instead, Elena uses the off-season as an opportunity to make a difference beyond the basketball court. She is an activist and campaigner for children and adults with special needs. She has written children's books where the protagonist is a little girl who struggles to come to terms with the fact that she is taller and different from all the little girls around her.

Single-mindedness and determination in sport are great, and throughout this book we have celebrated such tales. But there is more to life than competition. And for those like Elena, who have the courage to face this head on, the rewards have been immense.

'YOU ARE
WHAT YOU DO
NOT WHAT YOU SAY
YOU'LL DO.'

84

YOGI BERRA

Sometimes, it's easier to go along and not correct folks. Sometimes, it's best to let it go, to let people think what they want about you.

To many, Yogi Berra was best known for his quotes, malapropisms like 'It ain't over, until it's over' or 'You can observe a lot by watching'. The fact that he played most of his career as a catcher – perhaps the most physically demanding position on the baseball diamond, but also the least glamorous, and one few gifted players opt to play if they can help it – also contributed to the idea that he wasn't particularly bright.

Maybe his nickname didn't help. Born Lorenzo Pietro Berra, he was born in Saint Louis to parents who had emigrated from Italy a decade earlier. He went by Lawrence as a boy, but acquired the nickname 'Yogi' because a teammate felt he looked like an Indian yogi when he would calmly sit, arms and legs crossed, waiting to bat. He revealed the story of how he got the name long after retirement, but when your name is Yogi Berra, inevitably people will link you to a goofy cartoon character: Yogi Bear.

Indeed, when Yogi Bear was introduced in 1958, by which point Berra was an established star for the New York Yankees, he considered suing the character's creators, Hanna Barbera, feeling they were using his name. When

Berra passed away aged ninety, the Associated Press initially reported that it was 'Yogi Bear' who had died.

The list of Yogi-isms – quotes that raised both eyebrows and chuckles – is lengthy. Like when he said: 'Ninety per cent of baseball is mental; the other half is physical.' Or when he mused that 'It's déjà vu all over again.' Or this piece of advice: 'If you can't imitate him, don't copy him.'

He once gave directions to his house by telling a friend 'when you come to a fork in the road, take it'. When asked why he no longer patronised a particular restaurant, he said: 'Nobody goes there anymore. It's too crowded.' On the subject of funerals, he had this to say: 'Always go to other people's funerals, otherwise they won't go to yours.'

And yet when you dig a little deeper, many of his Yogi-isms take on more meaning. When he said 'It ain't over, until it's over', he was managing the New York Mets, a middling team who were way behind in their division and looked to have no chance of making the play-offs. Less than two months later, thanks to an amazing comeback, they won their division and advanced to the World Series. He was more than vindicated.

His lifetime achievements were impressive, and not just in baseball. At eighteen years old he served in the US Navy during World War II, participating in the attack on Omaha Beach and D-Day, coming under fire on both occasions. He later received several commendations for bravery in conflict.

Berra was named to the All-Star team in thirteen of his seventeen major league seasons and won three Most Valuable Player Awards. He won the World Series ten times as a player and another three times as coach and manager, all bar one with the Yankees. In many ways, the World Series he didn't win with the Yankees was his most impressive. The year was 1969 and he guided the New York Mets, a team formed just seven years earlier, to victory in the World

Series. To this day, that team is known as the 'Miracle Mets' because they were the ultimate no-hopers.

Post-retirement, Montclair State University in New Jersey opened the Yogi Berra Museum and Learning Center, the latter focused on teaching children about sportsmanship and dedication, two values that made him stand out all his life. And in 2015, Berra was posthumously awarded the Presidential Medal of Freedom by President Barack Obama: the highest honour the US government can bestow on civilians.

In time, people came to realise that his Yogi-isms, far from being the sign of a lack of intelligence, were quite the opposite. It may well have been Yogi messing around with the wider world all along. And even if it wasn't, why focus on words when his extraordinary deeds spoke such volumes?

Perhaps in the end, the truth lies in another Yogi-ism: 'I really didn't say everything I said.'

'WHEN LIFE HITS YOU, LOSERS SAY: WHY ME, WINNERS SAY: TRY ME.'

85

KYLE MAYNARD

Kyle Maynard won't lie to you. He won't tell you what so many motivational speakers will insist upon, that 'nothing is impossible'. Plenty is impossible. That's not what it's about. Rather, it's about discovering what your limits are and getting as close to them as you can. And, perhaps, being wrong and realising that your limits are far further out than you ever imagined.

Kyle was born as a congenital amputee, which basically means he has no limbs. His arms end just before the elbow, his legs just before the knee. To many people, this would make the most basic and mundane of tasks appear impossible. Yet, from a very young age, he drove himself to achieve them, through sheer willpower, repetition and application, whether it be using a spoon or putting on socks.

The first hundred times you might fail miserably. Then, in your next 1,000 attempts, you might get a small breakthrough. You build on that and, perhaps, after another few thousand tries, you get another. And then another. And then, at some point, you're eating with a spoon, despite the fact that you have no hands or forearms. Or you're putting on socks by yourself.

It's that mentality, which Maynard calls 'no excuses', that propelled him to wrestle throughout his time in school. Yes, wrestle. How could somebody who can't stand unassisted, can't grab hold of an opponent, and can't get any sort of full leverage from his legs even think of taking to the mat against an opponent?

The 'how' isn't an obstacle for Maynard. He finds a way over time. Indeed, he lost his first thirty-five wrestling matches, which started at the age of eleven. His father never relented, always pushing him to get back out there and do it again. And while his determination was tested – nobody likes to lose that often – Maynard never gave up. He found little advantages that he could gain, ways to minimise his disability, strategies to counter opponents. He won his thirty-sixth match after eighteen months of trying, which also involved driving around the Midwest of the United States finding tournaments where he'd be allowed to wrestle.

By the time he got to high school, Maynard wasn't a novelty or a charity case. He was a legitimate wrestler competing on the school team in the 103-pound category. In his senior year, he recorded thirty-five wins and sixteen defeats: a record most fully able-bodied wrestlers would be more than proud of.

At university in Georgia, he realised that beyond what he could do for himself – discovering his outer limits and pushing up against them – he had a gift for inspiring others. He became an accomplished motivational speaker, urging those with physical challenges to defy expectation and stretch themselves as far as they could.

Later, he climbed the tallest mountains of Africa (Kilimanjaro) and South America (Aconcagua) – and he achieved both without the use of prosthetics, bear-crawling up the mountains. You may have done a bear-crawl at the gym – but imagine doing it without hands and feet, and with limbs half as long as your own.

He knows what is possible. And he knows that, for those with enough perseverance, what is possible is a moving target. A target he will continue to pursue for the rest of his life.

'LEGENDS ARE BORN IN THE VALLEY OF STRUGGLE.'

86

NADIA COMĂNECI

The story is familiar to all, but it's worth retelling. The year was 1976, the venue was the final of the uneven bars at the Olympics in Montreal. Nadia Comăneci had just completed her routine to breathless, rapturous applause.

She sat, expressionless, waiting for her score. It flashed up: '1.00'. Given that gymnastics scores are out of 10, this was a disaster – and hardly plausible. An emissary rushed over with the news. No, it was not a 1.00. The judges had actually given her a perfect 10.00. The problem was the electronic scoreboard was not set up for more than three digits. Why? Because it didn't occur to anyone that the judges would ever award a '10.00'. Ten was perfection. And such a thing wasn't humanly possible in gymnastics. There was always room for improvement.

Or so they thought, before this tiny fourteen year old from Transylvania bounded on to the scene, becoming the first gymnast ever to record a perfect score.

Nadia would nail another six perfect tens in those Olympics, on her way to winning three gold medals, a silver and a bronze. Four years later, she would win two more gold medals, as well as two silvers.

The world of gymnastics was stunned. The wider world of casual viewers who tuned in every four years realised they were witnessing something special, a sport that would be changed forever – and it was thanks to a five foot, thirty-eight kilogram girl whose sad-eyed earnestness was disarming in its brutal, direct honesty.

'Yes, I can smile ... but I don't care to.' And 'No, I never cry. I have never cried.'

Those were two of the answers she gave in the routine post-event interviews, the sort where athletes generally talk about how they dreamed of this moment, thank their parents and coaches and talk about how happy and emotional they are. Not her.

Truth be told, the sport had already begun to change in 1972, when the Soviet Union's Olga Korbut won gold with routines that, compared to those of the past, were based far more on strength and athleticism than ballerina-like grace. But Nadia took it to another level.

She effortlessly performed moves that, until that point, had been pulled off only by men, like the piked backwards somersault perfected by the legendary Japanese gymnast Mitsuo Tsukahara. And she conjured up gyrations that nobody had seen before, of the sort that seemed to defy human biomechanics.

Korbut had opened the door to a more athletic form of gymnastics; Nadia ripped the doors off their hinges and performed the moves flawlessly. She and her coach, Béla Károlyi, reimagined what the sport could be. Until then, it had been an off-shoot of ballet or modern dance: graceful ladies performing well-worn routines. Nadia took it in an entirely different direction. Her small, light frame was a highly concentrated mass of powerful muscles, precisely those that ballerinas deemed unladylike. But she possessed a grace and a creativity that left audiences bedazzled at what they had just seen. Strong is beautiful. Powerful is beautiful. Flying is beautiful.

There was a dark side, of course. One over which she was, initially, powerless. Her athleticism was a product of her courage and work ethic, sure, but also a result of having been stowed away in Károlyi's de facto 'gymnast factory' from the age of six. She was raised to perform in the single-minded fashion that totalitarian regimes of that era, who understood the value of sport-as-propaganda, were wont to do.

And after the Olympics, she became something of a national treasure, used by Nicolae Ceaușescu's Romanian government as a symbol of pride and excellence. The attention became suffocating and the pressure only grew worse after Károlyi defected to the US in 1981. The Romanian government's paranoia that Nadia might do the same was intense. She was watched closely, and her travel was severely restricted.

Those were the darkest years of her life, torn between loyalty to her country and a desire to be free of her gilded cage. In November of 1989, with a small group of compatriots, she fled the country, on foot, walking through the wilderness overnight to Hungary and then on to Austria. It was dangerous and risky. It was the sort of journey desperate immigrants make, not Olympic gold medallists. But she made it.

Ironically, Ceaușescu was overthrown less than a month later and, had she waited until the New Year, she could simply have left of her own accord. It didn't matter though. Nadia had made her most important vault: to freedom. A few years later, she settled in Oklahoma and went on to marry Bart Conner, an American gymnast who she had first met nearly twenty years earlier at the Montreal Olympics.

Nadia had redefined gymnastics and taken the sport in an entirely different direction. How much of it was of her own volition and how much of it the product of a system that pushed young girls to the very edge (not coincidentally, rules have changed and now the minimum age in senior competition is sixteen) is something for others to judge. What she knows now, as a mother and an author (her book *Letters to a Young Gymnast* became a bestseller) is that she's truly free.

'ACHIEVEMENT HAS
NO COLOUR.'

87

FRANCOIS PIENAAR

One was a seventy-six-year-old black dissident who had spent twenty-seven years behind bars and been branded a terrorist by the government. The other was a six feet, four inches tall blond Afrikaner rugby star, who grew up in a thoroughly white environment, one where you were taught not to ask questions. Like, for example, why the aforementioned black dissident was, as was often repeated, such a 'bad man'.

A cloud hung over South Africa in the year or so before the 1995 World Cup. To some, it was a beneficial cloud, bringing the much-needed rain of democracy, equality and freedom to a parched land that had known mostly minority rule, inequality and repression. To others, the cloud signalled an incoming storm, one that would release decades of built-up tension and injustice and eventually lead to race-war.

Nelson Mandela had been elected president the year before in the country's first ever democratic election, one which saw black South Africans vote for the very first time. Even as the majority of the country celebrated their new-found voice, many in the white minority were fearful.

Francois Pienaar saw it all around him. The people with whom he had grown up, the privileged, sheltered elites, were stocking up on food, as if they were expecting Armageddon. As he put it in an interview with the *Guardian*:

'They feared that if this man who had been put in jail for twenty-seven years and was not handled particularly well as a prisoner, comes out, he's going to be slightly peeved.

'What he says, the nation will do,' he added. 'So if Mr Mandela came out of prison and said "Listen, this is wrong, we're taking the country by force," it would have been civil warfare. Then he came out and he didn't. The conservatives . . . [were] just waiting for [it] to happen. It never happened.'

That it didn't happen is down to Mandela's foresight and his understanding that healing had to be the nation's priority. That the healing was helped, in part, by what South Africa achieved at the 1995 World Cup is down to Pienaar.

South Africa had a proud rugby tradition, albeit one that was almost exclusively white. It wasn't just that most black South Africans preferred football; they actively hated the rugby team, the Springboks. In fact, they tended to support whoever was playing against the Springboks. The Springboks were seen as very much a symbol of apartheid.

Despite hosting the tournament, South Africa were far from the favourites going into it. Mandela knew that some, feeding off the age-old hatred of the Springboks, might turn an early exit into further humiliation, needlessly inflaming a situation that was already tense. So, he reached out to Pienaar, offering the rugby team all the support he could muster.

Mandela gave him and the rest of the team a quote to inspire them before the tournament. If you saw the film *Invictus*, you might think it was the William Henley poem of the same name, the one that ends: 'I am the master of my fate / I am the captain of my soul'. Well, that's Hollywood. In real life, though, the quote he gave them was no less inspirational. It was an excerpt from Teddy Roosevelt's 'Man in the Arena' speech: 'It is not the critic who counts; not the man who points out how the strong man stumbles or where the doer of deeds could have done them better.

The credit belongs to the man who is actually in the arena, whose face is marred by dust and sweat and blood.'

It was Mandela's way of getting them to exorcise the negativity around them, to make their own history. Whatever it might be, they were going to be a credit to the new South Africa. And he was entirely behind them.

Pienaar could have dismissed this as nothing more than empty words from a politician. But he took it to heart. And he got the players to respond in the same way. Among other things, they learned – and sang – the new South African national anthem, much of it written in languages other than their native English and Afrikaans. Pienaar also took the team to Robben Island, the infamous prison where Mandela was held for so long, reminding his teammates of the stakes and how a man 'could spend thirty years in a tiny cell and come out ready to forgive the people who put him there'.

The Springboks went on to win the World Cup, along the way defeating the heavily favoured New Zealand All Blacks in the final. Mandela, of course, was there, cheering them on, wearing a Springbok cap and Pienaar's green number six jersey. The bond between the two men was sealed forever that day. And South Africa, for all its challenges in the post-apartheid era – many of which still exist to this day – took a giant step closer to truly becoming one nation.

'FAITH MAKES THINGS POSSIBLE, NOT EASY.'

88

MARTA

Sometimes, it's about finding the door that lets you in. Or, more often, the crack that you can claw at, scratch at, until, little by little, you create first a hole, then a gap big enough to squeeze through.

Girls didn't play football in the town of Dois Riachos, up in the northeast of Brazil, in the flat countryside where Marta's mother worked morning to evening, before going to toil as a cleaner at City Hall. This wasn't something Marta learned from her mother, who wasn't around much: she was always working to feed her four children. And it's not something she picked up from her father, either: he left when Marta was a baby and never returned.

It was something that she picked up on in the air around her. The looks she got. The comments. The little sneers.

Her mother never discouraged her from playing football, but she never encouraged her, either. It's great when parents can be supportive of their children. But some simply don't have that option: they have to work, to put food on the table. As Marta herself recalled, her mother's message was always the same: 'Let her be.'

Kids learn from what they see and what they hear. And what Marta saw and heard, from the boys playing outside her front door and the games she saw on television, was football. Either men playing football or people talking about football. There was no escape. And she wanted to be a part of it.

And so, she played with the boys. She ran around barefoot chasing the ball until, some years later, the grandfather of one of her teammates took pity on her and gave her an old pair of football boots. They were worn down and ragged and needed to be stuffed with old newspapers so that her feet wouldn't rattle around inside them. But they were real football boots.

The fact that she was better than most meant she had her place on the local team. But being a girl meant she was *in* the team, but not *part of* the team. She changed and got ready by herself. It felt as though she was tolerated, not embraced. And when, as sometimes happened, rival teams refused to play against her because she was a girl, nobody on her team put up a fight. 'Sorry, Marta, you're going to sit out.' That was the message, time and again.

Marta asked herself that simplest of questions: 'Why would God give me this talent, if no one wants me to play?' It was, indeed, cruel. Or it would have been if fate – or God – hadn't also given her a lifeline. Thanks to relatives and friends, Marta secured a trial at Vasco Da Gama, one of Brazil's biggest clubs and, crucially, one that actually had a women's team.

One problem. Vasco was in Rio de Janeiro, some 2,000 kilometres away. It meant a journey of three days. And, once there, waiting several days for the phone to ring. Marta was fourteen years old. She had no idea what would await her on the other side, but she knew that she owed it to herself, to her talent and to her maker, who had bestowed it on her, to get on that bus and take that leap of faith.

Thus began a stellar career that would see her crowned as the Women's World Player of the Year no fewer than six times. She would go on to play in Sweden and the US, appearing in five World Cups and scoring in each and every one of them.

And she never forgot where she came from, or how steep her path up the mountain had been. After Brazil were knocked out by France in the Round of 16, she took the microphone and spoke to the world – more specifically to girls, and to the one she had been twenty years earlier.

'Women's football depends on you to survive,' she said. 'Think about it. Value it more. You have to cry at the beginning to be able to smile at the end.' Given what she had endured, she knew better than most just how tortuous the path was for women in football. And how, in many parts of the world, it still is. But those tears she cried at the beginning were not in vain. Far from it.

'EVERYTHING YOU EVER WANTED IS ON THE OTHER SIDE OF FEAR.'

89

GREG LOUGANIS

Going into the 1988 Seoul Olympics, Greg Louganis knew he was different. He could count the ways. There was the fact that he was adopted: his parents, of Swedish and Samoan descent, were both fifteen when he was born and had put him up for adoption. There was the fact that, as a little boy, he was into dance and acrobatics rather than sport: a function of trying to mimic his older adopted sister, perhaps. There was the dyslexia that was only diagnosed when he was at university. There was the depression. There was the heavy drug habit he had supported by dealing while in school.

He was different in other ways, too – much more positive ones. He was the greatest diver in the world, having won double gold four years earlier in Los Angeles in the ten-metre platform and three-metre springboard. And, in fact, he had been hailed as a diving phenomenon from an early age, winning a silver medal aged just sixteen at the Montreal Olympics. He had dominated the sport for more than a decade and knew he would have had even more medals if not for the US boycott of the 1980 Games in Moscow.

His was already a story of redemption and success. But during preliminaries in the three-metre springboard in Seoul, he attempted a reverse two-and-a-half somersault pike and hit the back of his head hard on the board. His body went limp as it landed in the water. He scrambled out of the pool, holding the back of his head, a mixture of water and blood oozing from his scalp.

Thirty-five minutes later he was back on the board, having received five temporary sutures and a warning from doctors, who feared he was concussed. He needed another dive to seal qualification for the next day's final, and he got it. Immediately afterwards, he was taken to the hospital, where the doctors sewed him up with permanent stitches.

That night, though, he felt very guilty. There was something he hadn't shared with the doctors, something nobody knew, apart from a few very close friends. A few months earlier, Louganis had been diagnosed with HIV and was already on anti-retroviral drugs. Had some of his blood infected the pool? Was he putting other divers at risk? What about the doctor who had sewn up his five-centimetre cut without wearing gloves? The guilt and terror hit him only later, in the hospital. Prior to that, the competitive adrenaline had locked his mind on to only one focus. But now he was questioning what he had done.

Today, more than thirty years later, we know enough about HIV to know that his worries were misplaced. Whatever drops of infected blood may have ended up in the pool would have been instantly diluted by the water, which, in any case, contained enough chlorine to kill the virus. Besides, you can't get HIV through casual contact. Other competitors would have needed to be diving with open wounds on their bodies and, even then, the chances of infection would have been infinitesimal.

Louganis eventually reassured himself. But the guilt hung over him on what should have been his day of triumph. He went on to win gold in the final the following day and, a week later, won another gold in the ten-metre platform as well, coming from behind to win with a reverse three-and-a-half somersault, one of the most difficult dives in his program.

A year later he retired from competition, and in 1994, he came out as gay. You could count on two hands the number of famous athletes who had willingly come out of the closet at that time. Louganis was easily the most famous male athlete to do so, and, perhaps the second most famous overall, after Martina Navratilova. Shortly thereafter, Louganis went further. By this stage, he had developed full-blown AIDS and he spoke openly about it. He also revealed his terror at the thought of having unwittingly infected others in Seoul.

'I wanted my story [to encourage] those people who are HIV-positive to be responsible and also to understand that life isn't over yet, that HIV and AIDS is not a death sentence,' he said. The courage it took to come out and reveal he was both gay and had AIDS probably paled beside the courage it took to admit what had happened in Seoul, and the terror under which he lived. But having his faced fears, he was liberated.

'UNLESS YOU TRY
TO DO SOMETHING
BEYOND WHAT YOU HAVE
ALREADY MASTERED,
YOU WILL NEVER GROW.'

90

MICHAEL JORDAN

Imagine being really good at your job. I mean, really, really good, to the point that the consensus is you're probably the best at it ever – and certainly the most famous. And then, suddenly, shrugging your shoulders, quitting and going off to do something entirely different. A heart surgeon who becomes a chef. A pop star who enrolls in the army. A CEO who decides he wants to be a schoolteacher.

Michael Jordan was thirty years old when he retired from basketball after nine seasons in the NBA. Nine seasons, in which he had been chosen for nine All-Star teams, led the league in scoring seven times, won three Most Valuable Player awards and led his team, the Chicago Bulls, to three consecutive NBA titles.

Four months later he announced that he was going to pursue a career in professional baseball. This was despite the fact that he hadn't actually played baseball since high school (and, even then, he'd quit just two games into his senior year).

Let's be clear about what playing baseball entails. As a batter, you have to use a bat, with a width of no more than 6.6 centimetres at its widest point, to hit a hard ball measuring just eight centimetres across, thrown by a man standing on a twenty-five centimetre mound some twenty metres away. If he's, say, 180cm tall, and you add in the length of his arm and the height of the mound, you're talking about trying to make contact with an object coming at you from a height of two-and-a-half metres (or more), often thrown at more than ninety miles an hour.

It's far from straightforward. Baseball players hone their hand–eye coordination over many years, which is why most don't make it into the major leagues until they're twenty-three or twenty-four years old. The vast majority of those who do make it have played baseball all through high school, then spent four or five years in the minor leagues or playing competitively in college. Jordan was picking up a bat for the first time in thirteen years.

But he did. He showed up at pre-season training with the Birmingham Barons, who played in the Double-A Minor League, a league two levels below the Majors. That meant swapping the glitz of the NBA and Chicago Stadium for ramshackle ballparks. It meant playing on teams where he was by far the oldest player (and, obviously, the wealthiest and most famous).

Jordan took it all in his stride. He trained with his usual intensity, taking extra batting practice before and after games. He continually asked for advice, not just from his coaches but from other players, too. He had the humility of someone who, above all, just wanted to learn a new trade.

His only extravagance? The team bus. Jordan was used to travelling via luxury charter jets, but Double-A teams travel by bus, sometimes for eight, ten, or even twelve hours. Jordan pulled some strings and – hey presto! – secured a luxury bus for the team: one that, according to reports, 'looked like a spaceship'. Beyond that – and the fact that he was one of the greatest athletes in the history of sport – he was just another Minor League baseball player, dreaming of the big time.

How did he do? He put up the numbers you'd expect from a guy who had tremendous athletic skills, but hadn't played the sport in thirteen years. His statistics were medi-ocre to average, but he showed potential. And he would have continued his hunt for a place in the Major Leagues, if not for the fact that professional baseball went on strike in the 1994 season.

With no baseball left to play, he returned to his 'other' sport, basketball, and duly won three more consecutive NBA titles, three more scoring titles and two more MVP awards. He took another break a few years later, then returned for two more seasons, playing his final basketball game at the age of forty.

When asked what prompted him to move into baseball, he simply said that he had 'fallen out of love with basketball'. Perhaps that was the main driver; or perhaps his move was a reaction to the murder of his father (who had been killed a year before he made the change), or maybe he simply wanted to test himself in another sport. Whatever the reason, he challenged himself and pursued his goal with the utmost humility. He knew he was the greatest on the hardwood floor, and he knew that he had to start from scratch on the baseball diamond. He was, above all, brutally honest with himself.

'I WANT TO INSPIRE PEOPLE. I WANT SOMEONE TO LOOK AT ME AND SAY "BECAUSE OF YOU, I DIDN'T GIVE UP"'

90+1

LUCA VIALLI

I guess it's up to me now. Maybe you know who I am. I'm a footballer, a striker, a guy who always enjoyed scoring goals. I played for Cremonese, for Sampdoria, for Juventus and for Chelsea, who I also managed. I won the league twice – with Juventus and Sampdoria – and I think I enjoyed the latter more. I captained Juventus to the 'cup with big ears' – the Champions League. I won every European club trophy, but Cremonese remains the club I love, while Chelsea is the club that moved me to London, thereby allowing me to meet the woman who would become my wife.

I live in London but whenever I can I escape back to Italy, to Grumello, near Cremona, deep in the countryside an hour or so from Milan. I seek refuge in the old house in which I grew up and which I hope my two daughters – both Londoners – will come to love as I do.

I like to stay in shape, to watch what I eat and to take long walks. Oh, and I play golf, and while I don't have a zero handicap, they tell me I have a decent swing, which has almost never caused me back pain or strains. But two years ago, while doing some physiotherapy exercises on my gluteus (for the less anatomically inclined, that would be my buttocks) I felt a sudden sharp pain, as if a small dog were biting my backside.

It's the sciatic nerve, they told me. Nothing to worry about, they said. It will pass. Maybe so, but for six weeks or so I could hardly sleep at night. I lost weight and I lost my sunny disposition. Eventually, I went for an MRI and they found a hernia perched above my nerve.

Rest did not work so I went to another therapy. This time it was injections of oxygen and ozone gas in the inflamed area. That didn't work either.

So, I call my old buddy Gigi Buffon. I remember that he had lower back problems around the time of the 2010 World Cup, in South Africa. He puts me in touch with his doctor, a luminary of orthopaedics in Milan. I work for Sky Italia at the weekend, then go to see him on a Monday.

I take my medical charts along, not sure what to expect. He studies them for a moment, looks me straight in the eye and says: 'OK, so we either wait six weeks and see if the hernia goes away, or we knock you out with a general anaesthetic and you go under the knife, right here, right now, and we take it out.'

I opt for the latter. Incredibly, the very next day I'm on a flight back home to London. Actually, that was against doctor's orders. At the clinic they told me I needed at least three days of bed rest. But that's just not me. If I'm going to rest, it's going to be in my own bed, with my family around me.

My wife tells me I'm crazy. And, for the first time in my life, I wonder if she's right. I start feeling a way I've never felt before. It's as if I've become someone else. I feel empty, drained, without an ounce of faith or positivity. I find myself crying often. I try to go for walks, but even a few steps are difficult. So difficult that I simply give up.

I am packed full of pills and drugs. I lose track of what they're called and what they do. Then, one night, I wake up with strong stomach cramps. I end up vomiting heavily. From that moment, I stop eating. I just can't. I'm in a permanently nauseous state.

All I can do is suck on liquorice. They tell me it helps. All I can see it doing is turning my wee into a dark, dense mess.

I'm scheduled to do some games for Sky, on Saturday and Sunday. I cancel Saturday, but grit my teeth, fly to Milan and show up on Sunday. Colleagues and staff look at me funnily.

'Are you OK, Luca?' they ask.

'Sure, I'm fine,' I reply.

But it's not true. It's a lie I tell them. I'm far from fine and I don't want them to know. That's why I wear a heavy, skin-tight jumper underneath my shirt. I want to look bulkier. I need to look bulkier. Because the real me, the one I see when I look at my naked reflection in the mirror, is a skeletal, weak version of who I used to be.

I go back to see the doctor the next day. On my way into the clinic, I notice a sign that says, in big letters:

'HUMANITAS'.

I think about it. I think about what it means. Let's talk to each other honestly and directly, looking each other in the eye.

Except my eyes are yellow. A pale, ugly yellow.

'You need to stop, or at least slow down,' the doctor tells me. He wants me to do another MRI.

Stop? Slow down? What does he mean? My life involves continuous pinballing from London to Milan, from Sky to the BBC, from friends to family to golf . . .

Stop? Slow down? What? Why?

I get the answer with my MRI.

I have cancer of the pancreas.

When he tells me this, I don't yet know that pancreatic cancer is one of the worst you can have. I just know that it's cancer, and it's bad. The worst is yet to come.

The doctor looks at me and says: 'Your chances are good . . .' It's the way he tells me, the way his words seem to blow out of his lips differently than they do when he's describing treatments and other diagnoses and cracking jokes, and the usual stuff doctors do.

My chances are good? Good for what?

I know nothing about biopsies and PET scans and lymph nodes and contrast mediums. I feel lost.

I go for my first biopsy. The lab technician says: 'Meh, you know what? I can't see a thing here. Maybe it's benign.'

I'm so happy that I start laughing. I jump up to hug him. (That must have been weird for him, as he told me that he was an Inter supporter and I'm a former Juventus captain.)

But he's wrong. It's not benign. Far from it. We need to move quickly. Surgery is set for a week later.

I go to Grumello to prepare. The landscape here is flat and agricultural, but I'm on a permanent rollercoaster. I tell myself to stick with what I know best. As a footballer, I had always prided myself on the way I'd prepare for a big match. I'd look after every detail, I'd get in the zone mentally, I'd visualise what would happen.

This is just another big game, like the many others you've played in, I tell myself.

I know I have a great coaching staff to prepare me: my wife, my sister, my brothers, my parents. They're old, very old, but they've aged well, like all my ancestors: longevity is our thing. We Viallis are made from sterner stuff.

That week, I sit down with my father and make him a solemn promise: 'I am not going before you or Mum.'

But I'm also a realist. I write my last will and testament. In so doing, I look at all the things I own for what they really are: things. Just things.

Yet I, and the people in my life, are something else. My wife, my girls, my siblings, my parents, my friends – all of us, all of you, are something more. We are thoughts and relationships; we are emotions and words.

We are the future that we can imagine for ourselves.

And so, I imagine that future. I decide not to tell my girls. The women in my life – my wife, my sister, my mum – are my accomplices here, spinning a web of half-truths and deception to insulate them from what is happening. My wife is simply extraordinary. She keeps everything together and still finds time to sleep on a cot next to my hospital bed for a week, just so she can be the first person I see when I open my eyes in the morning. And she's always positive, always upbeat, always relaxed. She acts as if we're in the second week of a three-week holiday in the world's best five-star resort.

My sister, too, is right by my side. She takes me to the surgery. It's 29 November. I note that it's the day that FC Barcelona was founded. I don't know why I think of that; it's just a nugget in my mind.

I'm ready. As the anaesthetic sets in and I go off to sleep, I keep telling myself: 'You will wake up again.'

I wake up. I have no sense of how much time has passed. And, try as I might, I can't open my eyes. But I hear voices. Mumbling, muffled voices. I hear them say the operation was useless, that it has spread everywhere: to the lungs, to the brain, to the stomach.

And so I scream. I still can't open my eyes or move my body – after what I'd later find out were nine straight hours spent unconscious – but I sure as heck can shout.

'I hear you! I can hear you! I'm awake! I know what you're saying about me!'

I can't see them, but I can tell from their voices they're shocked.

'Please, calm down . . . we weren't talking about you,' they whisper. I can hear their footsteps as they move away, and the sound of the curtain being drawn around me. At some point I go back to sleep, enveloped in a blanket of contrasting relief and worry.

When I finally do open my eyes, my wife is in front of me. There are tubes going into my body. Into my neck, into my abdomen. And there's a long, ugly surgical scar running down my front.

But I look into my wife's eyes and they look as if they're on fire: burning embers of happiness.

'It went well,' she says.

'How long do I have to stay here?'

'Two weeks.'

Yeah, right. I'm out in six days. Despite the protests of the doctors, despite their grim warnings, I simply can't stay. Not because I'm some kind of superman, but because I want to be with my family. I know myself well enough that I can't rest in a hospital. Once it's safe to go, I'm out of there.

My wife flies back to London, no doubt spinning more tales of deception for the girls, as ever wanting to protect them from the knowledge of what is happening to me.

It's my sister who takes care of me. And, in one sense, it's as if I'm a child again, being spoiled by my big sister. Some crisp mornings, when the winter sun peeks through the curtains of my room, it does feel as if time has stood still, as if nothing has happened and we're back where we were so many years ago. Christmas is approaching. I'm like a kid waiting for presents.

A week passes and she takes me back to get my stitches out. The hospital has already arranged my post-surgical treatment with a doctor in London, Professor Cunningham. He'll be the one taking care of me. He'll be the one who makes sure I'm fixed.

But first, there's Christmas. We're all together in London, at our home. I see my family in a way that I have never seen them before. On Boxing Day, I decide to tell them, amid the wrapping paper strewn through our living room.

How do I tell them? The same way I've told you.

As I speak to them, they start crying. I start crying, too. Through the tears I come to realise that cancer isn't an enemy to defeat. You are not trying to destroy cancer. It's a challenge: a battle against yourself.

In my case, it took me from the eighty-two kilograms I weighed back when I first did my physiotherapy and felt the little dog bite to now, when I'm just over sixty-six kilograms. When I finish telling my story, the house is silent. And warm. The girls are with me.

The worst is over. Now it's up to Professor Cunningham. And here, I'm in luck. He is one of the best oncologists in the world, with a great team. He works around the corner from my house – and he's a Chelsea fan! He's on board with the post-surgical treatment, and we're off: chemotherapy!

We begin on 9 January and continue for a full eight months. Three pills in the morning, three in the evening, and an intravenous drip, too. That is followed by six weeks of radiation therapy. My life becomes overwhelmed by side effects, hurled at me like bullets.

I know the percentage probability that the cancer will return, and I willingly ignore it. I'm a footballer. Anybody who has played will tell you probabilities are just that: chance. Whether it's one per cent or eighty per cent, you can't rule anything out. So the figures become meaningless. You just have to play.

It's a bombardment, all the same, and, more often than not, I'm numb and semi-conscious. I feel ill and, strangely, I feel ashamed, almost as if the cancer were my fault. I continue wearing the skin-tight jumpers under my shirts to try to bulk up, to try to look like what Gianluca Vialli is supposed to look like. Word gets out that I'm ill, but when people ask me, I play it down and only talk about the hernia. Even my closest friends are only told part of the truth, just one piece of the puzzle. This is a protective measure. To protect them, but also myself. The way they speak to me, relate to me, joke with me . . . I don't want that to change. Ever.

So, what do I do in that time? I do a lot of thinking, a

lot of reading, then more thinking. (Strangely, looking back now, I sometimes find myself feeling almost grateful for it – although I say this softly, and I emphasise the 'almost'.) Of course, I would rather have done without it, but it gives me the opportunity to reflect and to reorganise my life spiritually. I learn about Asian philosophies and find that they marry well with two qualities I've always had inside me: dedication to training (of all kinds, physical and mental), and optimism.

Fear turns out to be something with which I need to have a conversation, a dialogue. I'm talking about genuine fear, the kind that makes you lock yourself in the bathroom for hours so that your loved ones won't see you cry.

I ask Professor Cunningham if he believes that being positive and optimistic will increase my chances of getting better. He's a man of science, and he says 'Yes'. That's good enough for me.

In fact, it's all I need. I create a new routine for myself and I dedicate myself to it, body and soul. I wake up early. I meditate over mantras, short inspirational phrases. I seek out silence. I contemplate small, pleasant details, the sort you don't notice when you're always 'switched on'. I visualise my life a few years down the road, I work out, I write at least one positive thought per day. Many of them are now here, in this book.

I put on the skin-tight jumper under my shirt to bulk up my shape, and I go back on television, because I'm convinced that they need me. One day, when a journalist friend rings me up and tells me that rumours are rife that I'm unwell and goes so far as to tell me that he's been asked to write my obituary, I force myself to burst out laughing. Then I go back into training. Training my body and training my mind.

My muscles reappear. I gain weight. I start to walk and then run, I can taste my food again, I regain movement in my fingers. As for my mind, I seek depth in my thoughts. Or, better yet 'height'. I scribble positive thoughts on yellow sticky notes and stick them all over my office. I grow so familiar with these thoughts and quotes that I forget where I picked them up. It doesn't matter anyway. They are now a part of me. They are my spiritual strength . . . my armour. And so, too, is this book and the thoughts I have shared with you.

When the book was first published, in Italy back in November 2018, I noted that the chemo and radiotherapy were over, for now. And, sure enough, the following March, exams revealed the tumour was back. I knew it could happen, I wasn't entirely unprepared, but when they tell you the chances of your illness returning are relatively low, you tend to assume that it won't. Perhaps I'd taught myself - and been told throughout – that thinking positively really helps you not just to cope, but to survive.

It was a bit of a shock. Off I went for another nine months of chemo. Losing hair, but gaining a sense of vulnerability. Losing weight, but gaining a sense of uncertainty over whether I'd live or die. I know now that every time I wake up in the morning with even the tiniest ache or pain, that irrational doubt will plant itself firmly in my mind, without letting go: 'Is it back? Am I going to die?'

Physically, the second round of chemotherapy was tougher than the first because the drug levels were higher. Mentally, I tried to free my mind as much as I could. Meditation, sure, but also keeping busy. Which is why when the Italian Football Association gave me the opportunity to serve as head of the delegation at the European Championships, I accepted. If I'm thinking about work, it's easier to block the irrational thoughts out of my mind.

I don't see this as a battle. I am not a warrior. I am not fighting cancer: it's too strong an enemy and I wouldn't stand a chance. I am a man who is on journey and cancer has joined me on that journey, like an unwanted travelling companion. My goal is to keep moving, keep walking until he's had enough and leaves me alone.

The second bout of chemo and radiotherapy is over: for now, anyway. I don't know how this match is going to end – I'll only find out later. What I do know is that my team could not have been any better prepared and could not be playing any better.

They got the ball to me in a good position, with a clear look at the goal. I'm a striker; I'm right there. I can see it clearly: the goal, the net, the keeper. I know what I have to do. I know how to do it.

But the truth is that, when you aim for the goal, no matter how many times you've done it, no matter how often you've scored, it's always a little bit like your first time. You need courage, plenty of it. And also a slice of good luck.

I didn't feel that my work should end there, however. I would have gladly done without this illness, obviously, but I felt that my story and the others in this book could provide comfort to others.